COGNITIVE BEHAVIORAL THERAPY MADE SIMPLE

The 21 Day Step by Step Guide to Overcoming Depression, Anxiety, Anger, and Negative Thoughts

PUBLISHED BY: James W. Williams
Copyright © 2019 All rights reserved.

No part of this publication may be copied, reproduced in any format, by any means, electronic or otherwise, without prior consent from the copyright owner and publisher of this book.

TABLE OF CONTENTS

Your Free Gift 5

Introduction 6

Dealing with Overwhelming Emotions 9

Anger 12

Anxiety 15

Depression 18

Negative Thoughts 21

Cognitive Behavioral Therapy 24

Day 1: Get real with your emotions 28

Day 2: Put your feelings to words 33

Day 3: Talk to Someone 38

Day 4: Feel the music 43

Day 5: Take things outside 48

Day 6: Get Physical 52

Day 7: Give Yourself Permission to Heal 54

Day 8: Start Daydreaming Again 59

Day 9: Create a Gratitude List 64

Day 10: Meditate 69

Day 11: Pay Attention to Your Diet 74

DAY 12: Develop Your Own Mantra 79

Day 13: Practice Relaxed Breathing................ 84

Day 14: Gain Mastery Over Your Emotions.... 89

Day 15: Step Things Up with New Relaxation Techniques 94

Day 16: Reflect on the Experience 99

Day 17: Focus on the Good..............................104

Day 18: Uproot the Negative Sources 108

Day 19: Bring Positivity to Others...................113

Day 20: Live in the Moment 118

Day 21: Letting it all go 123

Embracing the Brand New You....................... 128

Closing 133

Thank you... 136

Your Free Gift

As a way of saying thanks for your purchase, I offer a free bonus E-book called ***Bulletproof Confidence*** as an exclusive token of gratitude to this book's readers.
To gain instant access, go to:

https://theartofmastery.com/confidence/

Inside the book, you will discover:

- A thorough understanding of shyness and social anxiety, as well as the brief psychology behind these issues
- Simple yet powerful strategies for overcoming social anxiety
- Breakdown of the key traits of a confident person
- Traits to DESTROY if you want to become confident
- Easy techniques to implement TODAY to keep the conversation flowing
- Confidence checklist to ensure you're on the right path toward self-development

Introduction

Do you ever feel like life seems to take extreme delight in brutally dealing with you as far as unfair outcomes? Do you struggle to sustain any sort of relationship in your life? Have you recently experienced an embarrassing emotional outburst that just seemingly happened for no particular reason? If you can relate to these scenarios, then you are not alone. Millions of people struggle with life daily and are unable to find healthy coping mechanisms. However, this book empowers and facilitates your journey to a brand new you that takes just 21 days!

Cognitive Behavioral Therapy made Simple: *The 21 Days Step by Step Guide to Overcoming Depression, Anxiety, Anger and Negative Thoughts* provides practical solutions for dealing with your emotions. As a result of each page, you will gain a deeper insight into who you are as an individual and why you probably act the way you do. This book will achieve the following goals:

- An in-depth analysis of anger, anxiety, depression, and negative thoughts
- The most effective methods used in cognitive behavioral therapy

- Simple steps you can implement daily to transform your life in just 21 days
- How to control your emotions and subsequently take control of your life
- How to be assertive without being aggressive in your relationships with others
- A practical guide for living your best life now

Many books that talk about cognitive behavioral therapy tend to be overly clinical in their approach and esoteric in their methods. In turn, these types of "medical jumbo jumbo" makes it extra difficult for the average person to clearly understand the concept, much less internalize the message enough to apply it to practical use in his or her everyday life. This book brings your common emotional problems to the forefront. It then breaks down the solution that is cognitive behavioral therapy, which essentially is all about putting you in better control of your emotions.

To ensure that you get the most from this book, there is a step by step guide included in the book for daily application. Those steps will get you from where you are now to exactly where you want to be in the future. There is no magic to it. All that is required is a little effort from you, and it starts by you simply flipping to the next page.

Ready to begin this exciting journey to a brand new you?

Dealing with Overwhelming Emotions

There are days when you wake up and you are super excited to take on the day. And then you have those occasions when you awaken, and you immediately regret it. It suddenly feels like the sun is too bright, the bed is too soft, the birds are chirping too loudly, and other people are just too happy. During those kinds of scenarios, the world feels unjust and cruel, and you would rather retreat to the confines of your duvet than face the world's injustices.

It may sound a tad too dramatic, but this experience is the reality for many people. If you are reading this book, perhaps you fall into this category. What you are experiencing is likely a myriad of emotions hitting you at the same time with such high intensity. It is like being struck by an airplane, except instead of having physical injuries, you get emotionally battered and overwhelmed. The world we live in today makes things even worse. The pressure to achieve so much in such a little time creates stress that is both toxic and damaging for your physical and mental health.

Nobody makes a deliberate decision to live his or her life in this manner. So, it is safe to say the people we surround ourselves with and the experiences we have had in life play a strong role in molding and shaping us into who we are and what we feel presently. Think of emotions as our psychological and mental defense mechanisms. When our bodies are infected with a virus, our biological defense mechanisms activate by creating antibodies to combat those viruses. In the same vein, when you have a negative experience, emotions stimulate to help you cope with the situation. If you are being attacked, you become afraid, thus fear triggers your survival instincts.

When you have been violated or unjustly hurt, for anger is stirred to help you stand up for yourself. But outside the regular natural response to life situations, if these emotions are activated frequently, they become a default setting: and when your default emotional setting comprises of negative emotions, your mind becomes a breeding ground for more negative emotions, which are even more dangerous than the initial emotion that generated the entire process in the first place. It is like a chain link. Fear begets paranoia which begets distrust that in turn begets anger, and it just keeps going. This chain of events takes you on a downward spiral that warrants external intervention to rectify.

When you get to that point where it seems like you are feeling everything, you are totally overwhelmed by emotions. Left on its own, you can quickly become extremely toxic. But don't despair, there is a solution. But before we get to that advice, let us look at some of these negative emotions and how much impact they have on our lives.

Anger

Anger is an emotion that has received a ton of negative press. In its regular state, it is an emotion that responds to situations where there is a perceived wrong. Sometimes, anger is in response to something done to you and in some cases, it is in response to something done to other people. The wrong in question doesn't have to be an actual physical thing. Words have a way of provoking anger. Perhaps your beliefs are being slighted and they can instigate anger in you.

People respond to anger in different ways. Because of the volatile nature of anger, some people opt to internalize their anger. This approach is a temporary measure, but the long-term effect could be just as devastating as a spontaneous outburst of anger. Anger, if left unattended and unaddressed, can simmer beneath the surface, thus masking its true intensity until a small and insignificant incident triggers a violent eruption of emotion. When you succumb to these violent compulsions, you end up hurting yourself and those around you.

When people are in the middle of these violent outbursts, they are caught in this haze that seems to rob them of control. It is like the flood gates of their emotions are broken, and everything just rushes in huge massive waves that sweep anything and anyone in their wake.

In that chaos, the person who is angry is unable to distinguish between friend or foe, adult or child, and in extreme cases, the violent expression of anger could be physical. But just as quickly as this haze takes over a person, it dissipates within moments. In essence, it can leave a trail of hurt and guilt.

People who are at the receiving end of an anger haze are not the only ones who are hurt by it. Those who express anger bouts are also injured by their actions and they are ashamed of it. This shame triggers guilt. And guilt, in turn, triggers anger, which leaves you trapped in an anger cycle. Each time you experience an anger outburst, you hurt others and feel hurt by the fact that you did. As a result, you feel ashamed, which brings you right back to anger again in a vicious cycle.

That said volatile anger is not the only form of expression. Some people are passive aggressive, and some people prefer to completely shut everyone from their lives when they are angry; and then you have people who tend to do a combination of different forms of anger expression. Whatever category you fall into, there is a way to get better control of your anger.

The goal is not to stop being angry entirely. Not only is that impossible, but it is also unhealthy. Remember, anger is like any other emotion you experience, which means it has many benefits, too. What we are hoping to achieve at the end of the book is to get you to a point where you can express your anger in a healthy and positive way. Because yes, it is possible to be angry, get the message you want to pass across and still ensure that everyone, including you, has a positive experience from it.

Anxiety

Like anger, anxiety is one of those negative emotions that actually acts as a defense mechanism to protect us. It is a biological response to stress. The concept of stress was probably reintroduced into the society about a decade ago, but it is something that has always been present for as long as humans have existed. If you are making comparisons, the main difference between earlier eras and now is the source of stress. There are numerous stress triggers in the world we live in today, and because of the way the modern society is structured as well as the advancements we have made in the areas of technology, these stressors are right in our homes. This would probably explain why stress is one of the most common mental ailments in today's world.

Stressors could be anything from your job, your relationship, your money issues to the actual real threat of danger. Anxiety basically helps you cope in stressful situations, and it is not to be confused with fear, which activates your survival instincts in situations where you feel your person is threatened. It is okay to feel anxious about certain things. It keeps you alert and helps you prepare for whatever it is that is making you apprehensive. However, when these feelings of anxiousness seem to paralyze you and prevent you from engaging in your normal routine activities, you have veered into an anxiety disorder.

Anxiety is often rooted in fear, and it can start making its manifestation from early childhood. Another cause of anxiety is an experience. An ugly incident that traumatized you could cause your anxiety levels to go into overdrive. According to researchers, people who come from families where there is a prevalence of anxiety disorders have a high chance of developing an anxiety disorder themselves because of the genetic component. Whatever the source of your anxiety disorder, it can have a strong negative impact on your daily life experience.

Like anger discussed in the previous chapter, anxiety is not an emotion that you want to eradicate entirely. Lack of any anxious feelings could lead to an even more dangerous mental situation for you with strong physical implications. Without any form of anxiety, it is easy to become reckless and show complete disregard for life. Without anxiety, you would sign up to jump out of a plane in midair, without paying any attention to safety precautions.

The goal of this book is not to stop you from feeling anxious. The objective is to get you to that point where you openly confront those hidden fears, and in so doing, you are able to take back control instead of letting those fears control you. With each step that you take in this program, you actively change the narrative that is your life, from someone whose life and important life decisions has been shaped by their fears to someone who is deliberately taking off the limitations placed on their lives. This is where we [by we, I mean you and I] get to witness a brilliant transformation and the only thing scary about it is the potential you have to lead a great and adventurous life that is only dictated by you.

Depression

Everyone experiences depression at least once in his or her life. The expression of it varies from person to person, although there are classic symptoms and the circumstances surrounding the depression go a long way to determine the intensity and duration of it. Depression happens as a result of immense sadness. That is not to say that every time you feel sad, you are going to get depressed. Sadness is the base level and at this stage, what you experience is a natural reaction to an event that caused hurt or loss. It plays an active role in the healing process after a traumatic experience.

But when sadness lingers on for too long, the outcome is depression: and when one is in this state, life becomes one of existence rather than of living. Depression manifests in people differently. Some people are unable to perform even the basest task. They remain their beds, unable to eat, drink or even function. It cripples their lives so much so that there is a complete lack of interest in living. Their mental health is unstable at this point as they lose the will to live. If left unchecked and unattended, they might give into to the lure of suicide, believing that only death holds the answers.

For some others, their own experience is quite the opposite: they are able to carry on life with every sense of normalcy. In fact, you might even find them laughing, joking and entertaining the crowd as the life of the party. But underneath that happy façade lies extreme sadness and pain. They use their joviality to mask their true state of mind. It is only if you are very observant that you would catch glimpses of their depression. And even then, they "snap out" out of their emotional vulnerability and resume their theatrics until they just can't bear the weight of their depression anymore. Again, if left unchecked, the end could be just as disastrous as people in the first group. The only difference is that no one ever really sees their actions coming.

And then you have people who exhibit a bit of both. One moment they are extremely happy, and the next moment they are down with overwhelming sadness. Many sufferers of depression also experience heightened anxiety and mood swings interspersed with moments of angry outbursts. Besides the emotional effect, depression also leaves its mark physically. Sufferers are likely to experience headaches and back pain in addition to tiredness. They feel exhausted all the time, have trouble sleeping, thinking and even speaking.

Depression peaks when the sufferer starts contemplating suicide. At that point, it is important to seek help immediately. The transition from sadness to the point of suicide does not happen overnight. It is a process that accumulates slowly without even the sufferer's awareness. Like anxiety, it can be inherited, so look up your family's history of mental health. With better knowledge, you are better able to fight. In the upcoming chapters, you will learn what your stressors and how to control them in such a way that they do not end up negatively affecting your mental health and happiness.

Negative Thoughts

We all have inner dialogues with ourselves. Our thoughts and opinions about events, people and even ourselves are prominent topics for these internal discussions. When you observe yourself in the mirror, it doesn't just end there with the glimpses of yourself. Your mind stores that information and then processes it. After processing the information, your mind links events and things in general to this information. For instance, if your favorite jean takes a tad more forceful energy to wear, your mind relates it to the slight bulge you saw earlier in the mirror and tells you perhaps, you need to cut back on the sweet foods as you might have gained weight. At this level, your reasoning is perfectly rational and within the normal limits.

However, things start to take a different turn when your mind starts pointing out absurd events that have nothing to do with the image it saw, and the links are usually very negative. For instance, if you walk into a room that was buzzing with conversation prior to your entrance and your mind feeds you with thoughts linking the sudden hush to your weight gain, that is negative. Perhaps you experienced a loss or were passed over for a promotion, and you start thinking it is because you are too fat, your inner dialogue has taken a very negative turn.

These examples are just trivial samples, but they articulate how negative thoughts work. The situations around you are processed internally and fed back to you in a way that completely demoralizes you.

Many people have been prompted to take actions that they normally wouldn't have taken by their consistent negative thoughts. Initially, you would reject the information you are being fed, but when you continuously meditate on those thoughts over time, you would start to believe them until they would almost become a reality for you. Harboring negative thoughts not only affects your mental psyche, but it can also destroy your relationships. This is because those negative thoughts affect your ability to objectively assess your relationships. Your reaction to those thoughts could vary. It could put you in a perpetual state of anger, which can spiral out of control. We already what uncontrollable anger can cause. It can also leave you depressed and unable to function at optimal levels.

In relationships where there is a complete absence of trust, the root cause is usually negative thoughts fed by events that have either been misconstrued or unresolved. It is mentally exhausting to stay focused on negative thoughts. It is like a dark cloud that blots out the sun leaving you unhappy and unable to take notice of the things that actually really matter. Such is the nature of negative thoughts. But as gloomy as this outlook is, it is very possible to retrain yourself to think in more positive terms. With consistent practice and deliberate effort, you can control how you process information and give yourself positive feedback. Cognitive behavioral therapy is key in this process and the next chapter explores how.

Cognitive Behavioral Therapy

Think of yourself as a slate that has so many words, images and texts scribbled over it in a way that makes it impossible to make sense of anything. You cannot tell where one text starts and where the other ends, but you are certain that they are all linked together in a way, but you just can't figure out how. If you were confronted with such a board, you would be saddened by its current state. It is not like a puzzle that you already have a clear picture of what the end product is meant to be. To make sense of this slate, you would have to get to the root word or foundational phrase. When you find that foundation, you may have to erase certain words and replace them with suitable alternatives; in sum, it is only as you piece each new word that you begin to see a semblance of normalcy. This process is what cognitive behavioral therapy encompasses.

When you find yourself acting, thinking and speaking in ways that you ought not to due to excessive anger, crippling anxiety, overwhelming depression and an upsurge of negative words, it would be impossible for life to make sense. This is because everything you do would be filtered through these emotions. It would seem as though everyone in the entire world is out to get you. Every step you take would seem to be steeped heavily in led. Little events spark up rage in you so volatile that it would seem you are carrying a little hurricane on the inside of you that is spinning everything out of control and destroying everything in its path. And it doesn't matter if it is raining outside or the sun is shining so bright, since you have your own personal thunderstorm complete with thick dark clouds and heavy showers that are programmed to flush out any happy thought or feeling. No wonder you feel the way you do. Your slate is completely messed up.

With Cognitive Behavioral Therapy (CBT), you start to understand why you feel the way you do. It is only in answering the question of why that you can determine how you can tip the scales in your favor. You did not wake up overnight and began to feel the way you do. Even if your condition is inherited, there are several behavioral patterns you have established over time that cause these conditions to set in. With Cognitive Behavioral Therapy, you can identify those behavioral patterns and offset their influence by deliberately replacing them with better behavioral practices that are more suitable. CBT is most effective in the mental conditions mentioned in the previous chapter. Although it has also been known to be used in the treatment of long terms ailments like irritable bowel syndrome which can be controlled by better eating behavior.

However, it is important to note that Cognitive Behavioral Therapy is not designed as a curative measure. Far from it. Instead, it helps you cope better with those conditions by effectively helping you take control over your emotions. For CBT to work, you will require the following in equal measure:

- Consistency
- Diligence
- Willingness
- Honesty

Within the context of this book, we are taking a slightly different route. Rather than sitting on a couch with a therapist, you would be going straight into the issues and taking proactive steps to resolve them. The goal is to help you establish new behaviors that you manage anger, anxiety, depression and negative thoughts. They say that it takes 21 days to develop a new habit. But that is not the reason we (you and I) are working with 21 days. I looked at these emotions discussed in this book and discovered that while our experiences differ, there are certain fundamental factors that can contribute to aggravating the situation. At the same time, there are specific behavioral elements that can be introduced to reverse the experience and bring you to a place where you are better able to cope with whatever is happening.

These daily exercises are very simple, but the effect is powerful. Some must be conducted repeatedly to have an effect. However, if done right, you can notice a significant difference from the first try. Others must be combined in specific scenarios for maximum impact, and I have carefully pointed those out as well. To get the desired results, it is important that you are deliberate in taking each action. It also helps to curate your experience post the action. This would help you put things in perspective and give you some insight into problematic areas. Remember the slate we used as an illustration at the beginning of this chapter. There is so much going on in your life right now, and none of it is probably making sense.

We (you and I) are using Cognitive Behavioral Therapy to retrace your steps, realign your behavior with the emotional results you are hoping to achieve and generally bring you to a place where you are emotionally balanced and content in who you are and the experiences you have in life. Because let's face it, life will always have those terrible and unfair incidents happen to us even though we are not quite deserving of those situations. But we don't have to let those incidences define us. When we root ourselves in our true identity, we will not be easily phased by what happens on the outside. There will be moments when you will slip. And that fall will discourage you from going forward. A momentary slip is not the end of the world. This is what makes you human. The part that makes you extraordinary is making the choice to get up from that fall, put the pieces that were broken apart and resolve to be stronger for it. You are made of more, and over the next 21 days, you will discover just how amazing you are!

Day 1
Get real with your emotions

One mistake that is a common practice among people who are battling with emotional issues, like the ones formerly discussed is the need to hide or bury their feelings. We are programmed to think that suppressing those feelings or denying them can somehow make those feelings fade away or disappear in time. Ironically, the opposite is what happens. When you choose to hide away what you feel, it simply stores away in the recesses of your mind. In that hidden corner, it continues to grow. And to facilitate its growth, it feeds off the other positive thoughts that occupy this section of your mind. There it will blossom and birth a not so docile version of the original emotion that started it in the first place. And at the next prompting, it will flare up and overcome your impulses causing you to react negatively.

This is why in some cases associated with anger, it would appear it is just a small incident that triggered the outburst. The fact is, that anger has been there for a while. It was slowly simmering beneath the surface giving you the illusion that by not responding to it the first time, you were able to squelch the feeling when the opposite was the case. And this applies to anxiety, depression and negative thoughts as well. The need to bury our emotions can be attributed to various factors such as our personalities or social upbringing. For instance, people who hate confrontation and act like people pleasers are more likely to not want to react in anger. If you have been angry in the past, whether it was your childhood or in your adult years and you were shamed for that display of emotion, the chances of you reacting in anger now or in the future are very slim.

This would also explain why many men secretly suffer from depression. You were told right from the time you were small that boys don't cry. So, even when you are hurt rather than respond to that hurt, you tend to bottle it up and stow it away. When I talked about depression, I specified that sadness is a very important part of the healing process. So, if you don't allow yourself to feel sad, you will most likely never fully recover from the pain. This goes on to sow a seed in your heart bears depression in full season. I could go on and give many illustrations on how we bottle our feelings and how the resultant effect could be the emotional instability that is being experienced now.

Hiding your feeling is a habit that needs to be broken immediately, and I can understand how this may not be something that you can deal with right away, but I didn't come here for halfway results. We (you and I) are going to do this now, and I will start by giving you a few facts to help you come to terms with the importance of this step.

1. Emotions are not gender sensitive.

Contrary to what you have been told, there are no emotions that are unique to gender. Being sad is not a feminine trait and neither is crying. If you have been hurt or are currently hurting, embrace the pain. Nobody likes to be sad. Not even the women whom you have been told are prone to sadness. But this is a part of human experience. The same goes for anger. Anger does not happen to you simply because you are of a particular gender. If your rights have been trampled on, anger alerts you to this. Sometimes, you may be right in that anger or maybe not. But this is not the stage to rationalize rights or wrongs. You are feeling it because you are human.

2. Emotions are not a display of weakness

I find it highly ironical that we are only able to discover our true strengths when we embrace our emotions. But this is the fact. Emotions don't just happen. They are activated, and those triggers alert you to things that are important to you. Surrendering to those emotions does not in any way diminish your capacity or potential for strength. Instead, it keeps you grounded in what you value, and it is when you are grounded that you can control your emotions. So, to learn to control your emotions, you have to learn to embrace them.

3. Emotions are unhealthy for you

There is no emotion that is unhealthy, and this feeling includes anger, anxiety, sadness, and even negative thoughts. It is your reaction to them that is classified as unhealthy. Anger helps you stand up for your wants and needs, sadness helps you cope with loss, anxiety alerts you to danger in your environment, and negative thoughts keep you from building castles in the sky. Denying these emotions would mean refuting these benefits and this what results in the problems you experience.

Now that you have a better understanding of the importance of emotions, you are now in a better position to embrace your real emotions. However, this is not license for you to go berserk. This chapter is not a do-all-you-want-to-do ticket. It is meant to help stay in touch with your emotions and controlling how you respond to them at the same time. Here is what you should do:

1. Find a physical release.

Mental rationalization is not always the best way to get real with your emotions. Sometimes, you need to do something physical to release it. Things like doing a workout, yelling into a pillow or even smashing something (be careful with this last bit) can help relieve you, especially when what you are feeling is very intense. This is why crying is very recommended. People say cliché things like crying doesn't help, but that is because they don't know better. It really helps.

2. Correctly identify your feeling at the moment

When you are in the heat of the moment, think about what it is you are really feeling. You may be looking at the person who possibly triggered your anger and thinking you hate the person, but in reality, what you are feeling isn't hate. You feel angry.

3. Direct your feelings appropriately

Perhaps you just broke up with someone, and you are in that phase where you think all men are scum or all women are horrible? Going with this attitude can breed anger, anxiety and subsequently depression. The right thing to do is focus on your partner who hurt you and feel what you feel towards him or her. Use this same strategy in all your dealings.

Getting real with your emotions can be a scary prospect, but when you get right down to it, you will save yourself a ton of pain and emotional turmoil in the long run.

Day 2

Put your feelings to words

When I was younger, I remember getting into squabbles with my siblings over the stupidest things and my mother would always intervene. I recall remaining angry and stone-faced right up to the point where she would ask us what happened. Then as if on cue, my voice would crack with emotion, and the tear gate would open. I would be babbling incoherently as I try to recount the event the way I recollect it happening. This happened whether I was the victim or not. Even as an adult, I have experienced this as well. Although I rarely ever get into altercations as much as I used to when I was younger, I have always noticed that whenever I was in a heightened emotional state and reacting to it, if I was asked to narrate the events that led up to that outburst, I always wind up extremely emotional. I am extremely certain that if you look at your history, this might be the case for you as well.

As a matter of fact, I never honestly realize the true extent of my emotions right up to that point where I have to explain it. This is the power of articulating your emotions. Now that you have taken the brave step to be real with how you feel, this next step is to help you explore the depth of those feelings. You don't have to do this in the presence of people if you don't want anyone to witness your emotional moment. This is not about anyone anyway. The objective is to try and discover how deep those feelings go. Sometimes, by articulating your feelings, you are given a perspective of the situation that allows you to see things objectively. You may be surprised by the conclusions this new objective offers.

For starters, in articulating your feelings, you might get to filter through your emotions and find out what is really putting the bee in your bonnet so to speak. In the heat of your emotions, it is difficult to see beyond what you feel but expressing them forces you to do so. Another surprising conclusion that you may come to is the fact that you may be making a mountain out of a molehill. That is not to say your feelings are trivial an don't deserve to be taken seriously. But in situations where emotions and tensions are running high, the slightest thing can trigger an unpleasant reaction. So, if you keep focusing on your reaction to this small incident, you will probably keep dancing around the issue without getting real solutions to the main problem.

This may feel contrary to the importance of staying with the moment, but I promise you that it isn't. If anything else, it is actually aligned with this sound advice. By articulating your feelings, you are able to stay in the moment because you are talking about what you are feeling right now. But it doesn't end there. This process helps you explore where those feelings are coming from, and I cannot emphasize how crucial this is for emotional growth and mental stability. So, now that we have established what this is about as well as its importance, how does one go about expressing one's feelings?

I can understand that this is not something that comes easily to most people. Already, you are at a place where it feels like you are experiencing a kaleidoscope of emotions and being asked to express them might require you to go deeper into those emotions which can be painful. However, you are going to have to apply the same courage, too, to embrace your real feelings to tick this off your 21-day list as well and when it comes down to it, you will find that it is much easier than you think, especially since you have faced down your true feelings.

So, to carry out this task successfully, you will need a journal. You could try using your phone or any other technology that is available. However, when using technology, resist the temptation to use emojis and emoticons to describe your feelings. Having those characters may look cute on your journal and perhaps cut back the time it would take you to articulately write out your thoughts in half, yet it also reduces the benefits you would have enjoyed by going through the process the prescribed way. A trick that worked for me was having two journals: one for chronicling my emotions in the heat of the moment and the other for when I wanted to reflect on how I felt about my emotional onslaught earlier.

Next, you would need to find a quiet time to do your emotional journaling. It could be at any time of the day. Just choose a moment when you can gather your thoughts. The location may not really matter much as long as you are able to sit quietly without anyone or anything disrupting your process for at least 15 minutes. If like me you decide to go the double journal route, you would save the quiet time for reflecting on your thoughts. When trying to journal in the heat of things, you would still need to take yourself outside of the situation and find a space for yourself. Don't hold back when you are writing. Your emotions at the moment may seem ugly, and you instinctively want to deny them, but we talked about the dangers of doing so in the last chapter. Embrace what you feel and write out your feelings in plain but honest terms.

Now, you don't have to be a poet to release your feelings. Although, if you happen to find yourself waxing lyrical as you jot down your feelings, that's fine too. We are not looking for perfection or the next book that would win the Pulitzer Prize. All you have to do is be honest with how you are feeling. If at the end of the day the words barely covered a quarter of a page or maybe you wound up doing three pages, it is fine. What matters is that the words there reflect the true state of your mind. Plus, I suspect that if you keep at this consistently (that is, writing out your feelings), the words would come to you much easier. Each entry would become more voluminous than the last.

The final stage in this process is reading what you have written. To do this, you have to step down from the throne of judgement as we have a tendency to judge ourselves too harshly. At the same time, you would have to take off any rose-tinted glasses you might be wearing. Honesty is a necessity if these steps are going to work for you. Objectivity is another requirement. You may be confronted with feelings of shame, guilt, and disgust as you read what you are feeling especially when reading the journal written in the heat of the moment. Let those feelings wash over you, but don't let them guide your actions going forward. And if you find yourself being overwhelmed by those feelings, it is time to take the next step.

Day 3

Talk to Someone

Our human need to interact with other humans often compels us to skip the first two steps and going straight for this stage. If you are lucky enough to have understanding friends who try their best to get where you are coming from and provide actionable solutions. In the very least, they would give you words that comfort and console you. The problem with this is that this only provides a very temporary reprieve from the emotional turmoil you are going through. And most importantly, there is a very high possibility that the conversation you had with them is one-sided and not honest. This is through no fault of yours.

Without taking the first two steps we recommended, you may not even be fully aware of what you truly feel. Your conversations about your feelings would skim the surface of your emotions without exploring it in its entire depth. And without getting to the root of the problem, your friend or whoever you confide in about these things may not be capable of proffering a solution that has lasting results. That is, unless you are speaking to a professional therapist who would help you sieve through the tangle of emotions to get to the root of what you are going through and even then, you will have to do the two things we mentioned earlier. The only difference is that your therapist would be guiding you through it.

You can only get the full benefits of having this talk with someone when you have come to terms with what you feel. Now, the purpose of this step is to get an external opinion on your emotional state. Again, this is not about judgement or seeking validation for what you feel. This is about helping you get past those dangerous emotions to a place where you can experience the true pleasures and joys of life. So, bearing this in mind, it is equally important that you are very selective about who you approach for this phase. The fact that they have been your closest friends for years or share blood with you does not automatically qualify them to take this important seat.

There are prerequisite qualities they must possess; and while I appreciate your desperation in seeking out someone to talk to, I have to emphasize that talking to just about anyone might prove to be more detrimental to your already fragile emotional state. Remember, we started out this journey to put a stopper on these emotions that appear to be taking over your life. Seeking out someone who is only capable of putting a Band-Aid on a bullet wound would lull you into a state of false security, thus leaving you to fall deeper into that emotional wormhole. So, to avoid this pitfall, be diligent in appraising the person you seek.

For starters, this person has to be someone you respect and who respects you in return. It is important to establish this from the onset because you are going to a place where you are going to be completely vulnerable to them. In your bare state, a person who has no respect for you would only be capable of seeing the flaws and not the potential for what you could become. And a person who can only see the flaws in you cannot in anyway proffer the answers you seek or even the companionship you need because he or she would only amplify the problem.

The person you go to has to be able to show emotional empathy. It is even better if you are aware that he or she been through a similar situation and have been able to come out of it. Emotional empathy helps them connect with where you are coming from without judgement. The absence of this would result in a talk down filled with criticisms and this is one of the last things you need. That is not to say the person dishing out those criticisms does so out of malice or hate. He or she just doesn't get your perspective.

Another quality the person you are turning must possess is honesty. We often trust people who we know to love us with issues like these, but it is very possible that the love that they feel for you hinders them or blinds them from being honest with you. In fact, their reaction when hearing what you are going through might be to bundle you up, wrap you in the fluffiest cotton clouds and then put you in a pain-free bubble where you no longer have to go through the things that you are going through again. These are good intentions but they do nothing to help promote your mental well-being.

Instead, you want someone who would face down those demons and be candid in his or her assessment. Be careful with people who are too honest though. And by being too honest, I mean people who blurt out the first thing that comes to one's head without thinking of the effect it may have on you. Honesty from a place of emotional empathy is what you need.

Finally, this person has to be someone who on some instinctual level you can sense that he or she has your best interest at heart. You have to have had some sort of relationship with him or her in order to establish this fact. And this relationship has to be based on trust. It may seem like you are asking for a lot when looking for all of these qualities in one person but bear in mind that your emotional well-being is at stake. Plus, if you pay close attention, that person may be closer than you think.

Perhaps a counsellor in your local church group, a close friend you may have known for years or even an older relative whom you are tightly bonded? In some cases, this person may be someone who you have a passing acquaintance-ship with. Just keep an open mind and if you feel there is no one who matches any of the criteria, go ahead and schedule a session with a therapist. He or she also in a good position to help you make sense of what you are feeling, and you can always expect a practical solution.

Day 4

Feel the music

I mean this bit quite literally. Music has an immense therapeutic effect on your mental health and not a lot of people understand this power. Before we go into how music helps you feel better, let us take a trip down history lane because contrary to what you think, music therapy is not a nouveau hippy concept that just sprang up. Its use and prevalence can be found in Greek mythology and even in elements of ancient Egyptology. The Greek god of the sun allegedly used music as a conduit for healing. Thus, it was widely believed that for one to possess health and healing, there must be a corresponding harmony in the music and what happens when the strings of Apollo's symbol, the lyre is in tune. Similarly, in ancient Egyptian culture, Asclepius, believed to be the son of Apollo, apparently cures mental ailments with music.

Leaving the realm of mythical gods and their powers, let us see the presence of music therapy in our culture. Native Americans believe that for all-round health, there has to be a balance of harmony between mind and body. When a member of the tribe falls ill, it is believed that this balance is out of order. To facilitate healing, the native shaman or healer would use a combination of herbs, potions and music. The music used is usually a blend of a song, dance and chance routine involving musical instruments and this music is often said to be inspired by visions and dreams. This takes us to one of the most depressing times in the history of humanity; the first and second world wars. Beyond the physical ravages of war, these battles took a strong emotional toll on the soldiers and understandably so. It was recorded that apart from the medical personnel assigned to treat ailing soldiers, musicians volunteered their services in hospitals. They went to perform their craft for the wounded, and it was observed that patients showed a positive response to these performances.

You are not deep in the trenches fighting with guns against an enemy seeking to destroy you as well, but the battles that you fight within can take the same emotional toll on you. And the casualty of this internal battle may not be on the same scale as a worldwide war, but you have just as much to lose. In essence, there is too much at stake to not take cognizance of any solution that is being proffered. Modern day music therapy has advanced beyond a song and dance routine. With the studies that have been conducted on the subject, the practice is much more deliberate and accurate in its delivery. But before talking about how music therapy works and how you can bring this into play in your situation, let us look at what the benefits of music therapy really entail.

For starters, it helps you redirect your focus from the emotional turmoil you are experiencing. When you listen to music, you become enthralled by the harmony of the sounds and this sensory experience transports you to another world where your current feelings or mood are shifted out of focus. This can immediately or gradually prompt you to change your mood. With the right kind of music, you are able to gain mastery over those negative emotions because right after distracting you from your pain, you are lulled into a relaxed state of mind. It is from this place that you can then start letting in the positive emotions enter. You can motivate yourself in areas where you previously felt you were unable to cope. And it is from this place that you can start feeding yourself with positive images that will counteract the negative images that you previously had.

Apart from psychological benefits, music therapy also has a good impact on your physical health. When you are stressed and experiencing anxiety at peak levels or perhaps you are in that anger haze we talked about, your blood pressure rises up as well. And when your blood pressure rises, your breathing is impacted as well. Listening to music can lower your blood pressure and help you regulate your breathing. And these are just on the surface. Including music therapy as part of your routine will go a long way in improving your mental health.

Music therapy is an aspect of cognitive behavioral therapy in that it helps you replace those negative behavioral patterns that have led you down the path to where you are now. By replacing those negative behaviors or thought processes, you can pull yourself out of the proverbial rabbit hole. Now, this measure is a step you are taking today, but like everything else I have included on this list, it requires repeated practice to obtain maximum results.

However, do not be quick to rush to your playlist just to listen to your favorite brand of music. We all respond to music differently and while certain genres of music may resonate deeply with you, the psychological effect may the opposite of what you are hoping to achieve. For instance, if you want to relax when you feel angry or anxious, listening to rock music is certainly not going to help you achieve that as it amplifies your feelings of anger and raises your discomfort levels. The same thing happens when you are in pain. Classical music on the other hand is known to have a soothing effect on the mind. If you listen to songs typically used in meditations, you hear a combination of soft musical elements like wind chimes, flutes and the likes.

But that is not to say that your options are limited to classical music and meditation chants. Certain audio books could also be helpful as could your favorite artists if their lyrics do not invite you. When you listen to music, observe how you react. This may clue you in regarding what kinds of music would work best for you. If your pain levels, anxiety and anger decrease, you are listening to the right stuff.

Day 5

Take things outside

One of the classic behavioral patterns that help nurture and groom an environment that dysfunctional thinking thrives in is the act of seclusion. Hiding yourself away from people and the world in general makes you more prone to thinking negative thoughts and basically living inside your head. You may tell yourself that, hey, you go out. You go to work, you drop the kids off at school, and you even do the grocery shopping in person. But, if you are honest with yourself, those actions do not necessarily count as "going out."

Many people like to use the excuse that they are introverts and feel more comfortable in their own space and so on. This is just that...an excuse. It is very possible to be an extrovert who attends every neighborhood party and has tons of friends who still engages in behaviors that are not healthy and part of the recommendation for changing those unhealthy behaviors would be to go out. "Going out" in this context is more than just routine practices or your interactions with people. What I mean here is taking yourself outside your comfort zone.

I can almost hear the crickets doing their thing in your mind after I made that last statement and I was totally expecting your reaction because it is perfectly natural. When we are confronted with highly emotional situations like these, it is instinctive to want to stick to the familiar for comfort. But there is a need to balance this experience of comfort with new experiences that would feed you thought process. Anger, anxiety, depression and negative thoughts are emotions that feed off your experiences, especially past experiences. They hold you back from enjoying your life in its full form. And when you are in this state, you are deprived of life's wonderful adventures leaving you to recoil back to those old experiences that feed the negativity...Do you see the pattern established here?

It is a repeating cycle that does nothing for your well-being. And since we are all about replacing old habits with new ones, you can see the need for going outside of your comfort zone. The prospect of going out into the world on your own can be scary and daunting. But if you continue to think of the world as this big place of unknowns, it will remain scary and I don't see you going outside with your mind in that state. Also, this is not saying that you should suddenly go from 0 to 100 just to get a new experience as that could backfire in terrible ways. Let us say you have a fear of spiders. Yet skipping all the steps to facing your fears and just heading straight to a museum of arachnids is insane and unadvisable.

Going outside here refers to doing things that are more in line with your interests. Say you have an interest in arts, attend an art exhibition. You can take things a step further by attending an art event that promotes a social change. Seeing people take this thing that you are interested in and use it to provoke positive change might just be the encouragement and inspiration you need to get out of your head. If your life revolves around work, take yourself outside the work environment. As a matter of fact, activities that are related to work should be avoided in this time frame that you have allotted to enjoying these new experiences.

It does not have to be anything grand. Skydiving is aspirational but let us keep our feet grounded for this one. Go out for a quiet stroll through the neighborhood. Stop and smell the flowers (literally and figuratively), observe the changing colors in your neighborhood. Catch a sunrise and watch a sunset, take a hike along the beach, go to your favorite restaurant and order something you have never eaten before. Stop and watch street performers do their thing, volunteer with an NGO, etc. This is what "going out" means. If you have the mind to make new friends, go ahead but that is not a prerequisite to this process.

This process is simply about doing new things. And if you find certain new activities more appealing, go ahead and repeat them. Look for things that bring joy to you, no matter how small. Things that make you feel relaxed without experiencing any of the feelings that brought you to this point in the first place should be encouraged. Apply caution with certain activities though. For instance, if the source of the negative emotions you experience is linked to your body weight, going all out on food splurge might have you feeling guilty in the end. And we all know how the guilt cycle manifests. Embrace your love for food but be conscious of the effect unhealthy eating behaviors would have on your weight and health in general. And then in keeping with the theme of taking things outside, look for a nutritional program that allows you to eat the things you want but in a healthier way.

Have a reward day where you treat yourself to a dainty dish that is tasty but still within the limits of what is considered healthy. It is a delicate balance but when you get right down to it, it is all about ceasing each moment and enjoying it. This gives you more positive things to think about. Bear in mind that some of these experiences may not turn out to be completely positive and this is okay. When that happens and you find yourself sinking back to that dark place, begin at step one and get right back to this point where you are ready to try out something new. Remember, new experiences create new thoughts!

Day 6

Get Physical

Exercises have tremendous health benefits and one of those benefits is a significant boost to your mental well-being. You may have heard incessantly because it is true. These benefits are experienced regardless of your age. The impact of exercises is particularly helpful for people who are suffering from anxiety, anger, depression and negative thoughts. And the best thing about this advice is that you don't have to suddenly become a fitness buff to reap the benefits. You don't have to sign up for a gym or get kitted up head to toe in sports gear for that matter. In essence, simple adjustments to the way you do certain physical activities are adequate to make an impact.

Exercises are not about running a 5k, doing a hundred bench presses in one sitting or doing some kind of impressive physical feat. Although, if you can do these things, that is good for you. It goes deeper than that. A short five-minute workout session can provide you with instant benefits. In fact, it has been proven that mild to moderate forms of depression can be treated with exercises. The effectiveness of these exercises on this form of depression is akin to taking anti-depressant medication and the best part about it is that you do not get the side effects associated with the medications. When it comes to anger and anxiety, I feel like this is a no brainer as exercise provides an outlet for those emotions. You hear people say things like they are going to let off some steam. This is exactly what exercises do for emotions like these.

With each movement of your body, you are releasing the internal tension you feel: and by the time you are done, the worst of the storm has passed. This correlation is because when you exercise, the body releases endorphins in your brain. Endorphins are also known as the happy hormones. They help cause you to relax and improve your mood. Also, let us not forget the mind-body connection that was discussed when we talked about music therapy. Exercise puts your body in alignment with your mind, hence causing you to focus. The combination of all these benefits results in an overall healthy state of mind.

After hearing all the great things that exercise ca do I can see how you want to rush to the nearest gym. However, if you have not engaged in physical exercise for a while, you might want to start off really slow. This would give your body some time to adjust to the process. You might experience muscle aches and body pain after the first try. Take baby steps and let your body guide you.

Day 7

Give Yourself Permission to Heal

In my experience, no matter how selfish we are in our actions or even in our dealings with others, we are most critical when it comes to dealing with ourselves. Even people who have a tendency to pass the blame to anyone but themselves still find that they are trapped in a cycle of self-loathing. And if left unchecked, that self-loathing quickly grows into dark emotions that paralyzes them and binds them to living a life that can only be described as hellish. This is even worse for people who tend to be people pleasers. Because their confidence is attached to their ability to ensure that everyone around them is happy, every failure becomes a red marker in their psychological ledger and continues until their emotional scars are torn, which causes tremendous psychological pain. And this pain leads us to where we are today.

One of the many truth nuggets throughout this book is that it is impossible to please everyone. Even *you cannot please you* 100% of the time. Accepting this truth is vital to helping you with the subject matter of this chapter. You should also note that failure to please someone does not diminish your value or sense of worth. Now that we have laid the foundation for this chapter, let us go in depth into what you need to do today.

I have no idea what pain you have lived through today. I don't know of the emotional battles and the psychological war that rages within you. I have had my fair share of pain: and while you may be able to empathize with my pain and vice versa, it is safe to say that our scars are different. Pain is a part of human existence. At some point, you will be hurt, you will lose someone you care deeply about and you will feel acute pain that has nothing to do with your physical person. But along with that pain accompanies the prospect of healing. It is life's way of keeping the balance.

When you scar physically, almost immediately, the healing process is activated. You may still feel the pain over a few hours, days or weeks depending on the extent of the injury. But it does not negate the fact that healing is happening somewhere underneath it all. However, there are certain things that could slow down or completely halt the healing process. If the wound is not cleaned and treated properly, it could become infected and worsen the state of the wound. In some instances, you would need to cover the wound to protect it from outside elements that might contaminate the wound and trigger an infection. For injuries that are very complicated, you may have to seek out professional medical options to facilitate healing. All of these processes apply with psychological injuries, too.

When you suffer psychological trauma, the shockwave of pain and other elemental emotions such as fear, anger and sadness alert you to this. These primary emotions could be experienced for hours, days or weeks and like the physical injuries we discussed, the timespan would depend on the extent of the trauma. Plenty of us have a tendency to get frustrated at this point and who can blame you? Emotions like these force you to relive the moments leading up to and during the trauma and each replay is worse than the actual event that occurred. If you are in this phase, it is time to cut back on any activity or thought process that you engage in that feeds the habit of blocking out your feeling. Think of it as cleaning the wound so to speak. When you want to clean and disinfect a physical injury, the chances are it will hurt. But if you skip that process because you want to avoid the hurt, you leave an open door for infections and we all know how that would end.

Accept that pain is necessary for healing. Accept that you are not going to get back to feeling "normal" overnight. Accept that what has happened while utterly tragic and unfair has happened and you cannot change that. Now when you have opened yourself to this, there are things you shouldn't do to ensure that these acceptances keep the door open for healing. It is tempting to want to skip to the future where your pain becomes completely numb or a dull throb at the very least. Don't. At least not today. Focus on the right now. Look at the progress you have made in the last few days. Acknowledge the successes you have achieved.

This helps to affirm the fact that you are in control of these emotions and not the other way around. Things may have happened to you, but now you have chosen to happen to things. If you are confronted with images, words or events that remind you of the trauma you have just lived through and your emotional experience takes you to ground zero where it feels like you are reliving everything all over again, resist the urge to question your progress. It is like poking the area around the wound every 5 minutes and wondering why you still feel the pain. You need time to heal and you need to give yourself permission to do just that.

Everyone has his or her own healing pace, regardless of the extent of the trauma. What is important for you to do is to put aside your expectations of your healing timeline and focus on the progress you are making. It can get pretty frustrating because sometimes it is hard to see how far we have come; but in truth, each step you take on this journey takes you farther away from the darkness that threatens within. You just have to remind yourself that the person you are today is better than the person you were yesterday.

For deep and painful wounds, healing begins on the inside in places we cannot see but as time progresses, you begin to notice the difference on the surface. The same philosophy applies here. Be patient and stay true to the process.

Day 8
Start Daydreaming Again

Remember those days long before the darkness took over your mind and your life...time when you would sit back and dream of an alternate life featuring a better you and all of those elements in life that you cannot exactly pinpoint? But somehow, they just complete you. Recall how you would dwell on those dreams and have a silly grin on your face? Those were the good old days yeah? Those dreams have become something relegated to the back of your mind or the bottom of your to-do list by adulthood and life's treacherous experiences. They may seem like relics from a past that you no longer wish to acknowledge. Perhaps, they symbolize your failures or remind you of how silly you once were?

But believe it or not, that silliness is exactly what you need now. Part of the root cause of the emotional trauma you are experiencing is the fact that you have chosen to put your focus on the unpleasant experiences you have had. Some of us give the excuse of "being real." Under the guise of being realistic, we deprive ourselves of the simple pleasures of daydreams and choose instead to align our thoughts with constant reminders of the darkness from our traumas. This behavior traps us in an endless cycle of gloom and depression.

When you talk about daydreams, people think of escapism. A dodgy way to disconnect yourself from the responsibilities of the present and immerse yourself in a world that does not exist. And we cannot dismiss these worries. Many people have been led down the wrong path with their daydreams and fantasy so you would be right to apply caution. However, most creatives, inventors and innovators harness the power of daydreams to renew their sense of purpose, motivate themselves and develop new solutions. You may not be in any of these three categories, but we are going to use the techniques these pioneers used to get to the next stage in this process.

For creators and innovators, using visualizations and daydreams provides a roadmap to where they want to go or what they hope to achieve by setting an aspirational tone. For instance, a novelist would visualize her book's characters in detail. These particulars are usually so vivid that at the end of it, this completely fictional character has a birthday, personality quirks and whole other attributes that when she talks about them in her book, so it becomes almost difficult to determine if those characters never existed in the first place. Today, you are going to do the same thing. Of course, there will a few differences when you look at how the novelist goes about writing her stories, but the objective will be the same.

Instead of thinking of it as indulging in fantasies, approach it instead as you are re-writing your story. Go to that moment hurt or traumatizes you the most. It is a painful journey to take, but it is a necessary one. Now when you get to that moment, in place of replaying the victim role, be more assertive. This is your imagination at work, you are in complete control. So, take back the power that was taken away from you. This does not alter the physical reality of what has happened but the impact of this process on your psyche is tremendously beneficial. And these benefits can extend into the physical aspects of your life. If you are looking for more reasons to start daydreaming today, here are a few:

1. Psychologists believe that these do-over daydreams as they are often called have the power to provide both relief and release when you are actively trying to resolve issues of anger, guilt and frustration over a traumatic emotional experience. Essentially, they help you let off steam.

2. Daydreaming is a form of self-hypnosis albeit in a very minute capacity. If channeled correctly, you can use it to change your perception about certain scenarios. In fact, it is so powerful that you can integrate it to alter behavioral patterns that you feel or are very certain has an adverse effect on your mental health. For a program that seeks to help you

transform your life in just 21 days, this is very important.

3. Indulging in daydreams can make you happier as a person. This approach is because, through the alternate reality you have created, you are able to envision what you want and if those dreams are rooted in positive seeds, you inspire yourself with renewed hope. Over time, this hope would nurture an enthusiasm for life that will eventually pull you from any depression.

These benefits are culled specifically for you but there is so much more to daydreaming than what I have listed here. If revisiting the event that traumatized you feels overwhelming, you could try focusing on the kind of future you would want for yourself. For instance, you might try picturing scenarios that got you upset and angry. Say an altercation with a colleague at work. Now, try as much as possible not to play out a revenge scenario where you empower yourself with this superhuman strength that enables you physically defend yourself, halt the offending colleague in his or her tracks and at the same time impress the rest of your co-workers.

This kind of fantasy might leave you feeling temporarily good, but it does nothing to correct the kind of behaviors that get you into trouble in the first place. The focus of the daydream should be on a specific behavior. Let's say you have a tendency to lay back when you are being attacked. Perhaps you have talked yourself into believing that this behavior helps keep the peace? On the surface, what this does is ensure that that you avoid getting into altercations or situations that make you displease people further. This would leave you with unresolved feelings of anger, shame and if unchecked, depression.

The ideal daydream for this would be a scenario where you speak up for yourself. At first, you would get a rush of relief from this and then with consistent practice, you will get to the point where you are emboldened enough to speak out in real life scenarios. And that dear reader, is the point of the process to get you to take a more active role in the transformation of your life. Your imagination and thoughts have played a major in contributing to your emotional turmoil. Today, you are taking over the reins, redirecting your thoughts to a more positive path and wielding the power of thoughts in the transformation of your life. I am getting excited just thinking about the great things you can achieve from here.

Day 9

Create a Gratitude List

This bit is pretty straight-forward, but the impact on our lives is tremendous. You see, the foundation of the negative thoughts that stir us in the wrong direction emotionally is our focus on things that we feel we should have, but we do not. These things are not always material. It could be the love and full attention of a partner, the ideal job that doesn't take too much from you pays you oodles of money and plenty of vacation time and the list goes on. Sometimes, it could be something as simple as hearing the person who hurt you so bad offering a genuine heartfelt apology.

We focus so much on these things we want to have that despite the things we do have, we are rendered impotent and incapable of moving on because we have associated our sense of worth with what we do not have. Without that job, you cannot be a competent provider for your family, without that apology you cannot move on with your life, without the attention of your spouse, you feel unloved and unwanted. So, we justify our negative emotional state with the absence of these things that we crave. I know that you cannot see this now but as long as you are alive, you are standing on the precipice of great and wonderful possibilities every day that you are awake.

Happiness is at your door. All you have to do is open that door. However, when you continue to dwell on the have-nots and value yourself accordingly, you close yourself off to whatever chances you may have at happiness. If you are the spiritual sort, your prayers become an endless loop of requests for those things that you desire and when you do not have them, you become disappointed. And when this happens on a daily basis, you have just bought yourself a one-way ticket to Depression-Ville.

If you have taken every step of this journey so far, you will discover a common pattern. A truth that is obvious but not many see. The fact that the power to change all of this is in you. You hold the key. It is not the job that you seek that is going to change your life. The money that it pays would provide some amazing experiences and perhaps make life a little easier to handle, but I can guarantee that even if you are offered this job in the next three seconds, your happiness will not last beyond the first paycheck. And this is because the job is just a quick fix, like a Band-Aid for a surgical wound. The genuine source of happiness that can take you through life is in you and thankfully, this is something that you already have.

I can almost hear the gears shifting in your head. "Me?", you probably wonder. Well the answer is an emphatic yes. Your happiness is in you. Again, let us not distract ourselves with the have-nots. But I have a pot belly, I am overweight, if only I were thinner etcetera. Those are irrelevant. I have been privileged to know amazing people who were rendered completely incapacitated by debilitating physical ailments and yet, even in their paralytic state, they were able to find joy and happiness. Their joy was so contagious that the moment you came into their presence; you cannot help but be infected by it. So, whatever it is you are going to say is just an excuse. And you have got to stop making excuses. You are more than that!

Instead of focusing on the have-nots, try to be more conscious of what you do have. I can understand and even empathize with the tragedies you have had to survive in your life, but we are past those hardships now. They have happened or may be happening, but so is the good stuff. There are many good things going on in your life every day if you know where to look. One thing that helps points us in the right direction is the gratitude list. As I mentioned earlier, this is pretty straight-forward. It is simply a list of things that you are grateful for each day.

Items on your gratitude list do not have to be grand. And it doesn't have to be mundane, either. It should be things that you are genuinely grateful for. You don't have to look too far for these things. I have this yellow flower pot in my garden. I have a mix of flowers in them and when they are in bloom, it just lights up the entire space. Even when the flowers are not in bloom, this quirky pot makes a striking feature that just lifts my spirits when I see it. This pot always makes it on my gratitude list. My garden and the moments I spend there would definitely be duller without it. Another thing that makes my list if I see it is a sunrise. It doesn't matter if it is a spectacular Instagram worthy type of sunrise or just this bright light gradually peeking from the skies, I am always moved when I witness one. It is like seeing the birth of the day.

These are just a few samples of what makes it to my list. Of course, it is much more extensive than that. But whether it is a smile from a stranger, a pat on the back or the fact that you were able to complete a task, as long as you derived some sort of joy from it no matter how small, it should make its way to your gratitude list. No matter how grim your situation is, look for those little rays of lights and record them. Before you begin your list, you need to get the right type of journal. It doesn't have to be grand and fancy, but it should be visually stimulating enough to get you excited about filling its pages with the things you are feeling grateful for. You can take a bland journal and personalize it. The more personal the journal feels to you, the higher the chances are that you will use it frequently.

When you have purchased the journal, set aside a specific time of the day to make your journal entry, make a ritual of it if you will. I like to do it towards the end of the day by the pool while I enjoy my cigar [it is an expensive habit, but it is one of my very few indulgences). Pick a time when you feel more relaxed and less distracted. Turn off your phone, have a favorite dessert nearby, put on some music. Basically, anything that puts you in a good place. Then you make your entry. Don't panic if you can't fill a page on your first entry. It might take a while to get into the habit, but keep at it. Consistency is key. And before you talk yourself out of doing anything, hang in there and really look deeply. There are tons of things that you can appreciated. You only need to look closely.

Day 10

Meditate

For someone who has lived in one's head for quite a while, the thought of spending more time inside there might not seem like the ideal solution especially given the negative situation of things up there. But, to make the advancement to the next stage, meditation is a necessary part of the process. I believe that the misconceptions people have about meditation are based on what the media feeds us. We hear meditation, and we think images of a person wearing white and sitting on a spot with a good view of the sun oom-ing and ah-ing to the chants of crystals clanging somewhere in the background — not a very relatable image, I must say.

Meditation is more than just the rituals the new age enthusiasts have pedaled in order to sell the idea to the rest of the world. It is a combination of breath control techniques that help us to consciously channel our inner thoughts and regulate the tide of our emotions bringing us to a place where we are completely relaxed, focused and in control. The objective of this exercise is not control although it is a desirable outcome. The ultimate goal is focus.

When you are in a highly emotional state, you are drawn in a million different directions. You become lost in the sea of emotions you are experiencing and are unable to focus on what is important. Being in this state can cause you to take actions that have no valuable benefit to you whatsoever. Meditation pulls you from this brink of confusion by creating what I like to think of as an imaginary pipeline that allows those emotions to seep out and then bring you to an emotional ground zero where you can begin to isolate the cause of the problem before reacting to it objectively. You are able to do all of these with guided breathing among other techniques which will be included as you advance.

The mental benefits of meditation are infinite, but I will stick with the ones that really stand out in context of your current situation:

It improves mental clarity.
1. It is effective in drawing out the negative emotions that affect your day to day living.
2. It enables you to identify the real truths in your situation.
3. It helps you stay more organized.
4. It prevents you from making irrational decisions in the height of your emotional turmoil.
5. It offers you more control over emotions like anger and depression
6. It allows you to cope with the emotional aftermath of extremely traumatic events.

Meditation is not just the fad of the moment. Elements of it can be found in just about any religion so, you do not have to be concerned about imbibing foreign cultures that may violate your own personal beliefs. Meditation may be an active ritual for the Buddhists, Hinduists and others, but we can all benefit from using it. The difference is how we segue into it. Some people require chants, incense, lit candles and a specific outfit to do it, but you can reap the full benefits of meditation without having to go through those rituals. All you need is a quiet place that enables you to calm your thoughts and focus on your breathing.

Meditation is not determined by the time of the day, either. You do not need sunrise or sunset or even the time of the day when the sun is at its peak. What you need is the time of the day when you can hear your own voice the loudest. If you are single, live alone and you work from home, you have all the time in the world to yourself. For married folks with kids, determining the precise time may be a bit trickier. Right before the household awakes and you begin your day might be a perfect time. The house is quiet and the activities needed to get things along can wait a few more minutes. Use this time to meditate. Some people may prefer the end of the day when all is said and done and everyone has crawled into bed to rest for the night. The only problem that I see with this is that you might be too exhausted to really get into meditation mode.

I have a friend who is a stay at home father. He swears that his perfect meditation time is somewhere between 10 and 11. Everyone has left the house, the basic chores are done and he has even done a quick check for those important emails. So, instead of using that time to follow up on the rest of his chores or work, he meditates. This just goes on to illustrate that the best time of the day is not dependent on the hour or the direction of the sun.

Now that you have sorted out your meditation time, the next thing is to set the tone for it. Some people like the bright light, hence the importance of the sun for them. I like lights too, but when they are too bright, they distract me. Instead, what I do is draw the curtains closed, turn off all the lights and take out a candle. I like scented ones because they relax, me and the light of the candle helps me to focus my thoughts. If you are at work, you may want to do your meditation around lunch time when things generally slow down and people generally go out for lunch.

The next thing to consider is the duration of the meditation. One hour, 30 minutes, ten minutes... No amount of time is too long or too short. As long as it does not interfere with your regular routine and it is done right. For a beginner or a really busy person, you can start with 5 minutes a day. As you begin to reap the benefits, you can increase that time limit to what suits you. Just ensure that you are getting the most of your time. After picking the ideal time of the day that works for you, the next step is to pick a spot. Again, nothing grand is required. You can do it on your bed. Just make sure that it is an uncluttered space that offers a little privacy.

Next, choose a meditation position. You can choose to lie down, sit down or go for the more traditional meditative pose if you are more comfortable with it. Most people have a tough time getting through the next part which essentially involves you sitting down for a period without thinking. There are meditation tapes and apps to help you with that. Or you can just light a candle and fix your gaze on it. Let all your thoughts and feelings be directed towards the candle. Do this consistently for a few days and you would begin to experience a clutter-free mind, even if it is just for a few minutes a day.

Day 11
Pay Attention to Your Diet

There is a popular saying, you are what you eat. Many fitness enthusiasts and experts have translated this to imply that your physical health is determined by what you eat. While this is true, things are a lot deeper than that. Your diet is instrumental in your emotional and mental well-being. There are studies that have indicated that people on a diet that is rich in vegetables, fruits, beans, fish as well as unsaturated fats like olive oil are less inclined to suffer from depression. This research barely covers the surface of what could potentially be a revolutionary approach to resolving mental issues.

Granted, it would be inaccurate to suggest that whatever mental and emotional health issues we have are a direct result of the type of food we eat, we cannot be dismissive of the important role that our food plays in contributing to our state of mind. There situations where people develop an unhealthy relationship with their food. There is a reason why certain foods are labelled comfort foods. They feed our emotional needs at the time. When we are experiencing certain emotions, we lean on these comfort foods to help us feel better. Many, these so-called comfort foods are not 100% healthy in the first place. Gorging on them in a bid to alter our negative emotional state would only amplify the negative effect these foods would have. And it is this unhealthy emotional dependency on food that has caused severe health complications for some people.

Food addiction can result in obesity, high blood pressure, diabetes and even heart diseases. People who struggle with food addiction also find themselves struggling with poor confidence, depression and low self-esteem and this battle tosses them into the continuous cycle that starts with poor emotional health and then leads l to poor eating habits that cause health complications and then brings them back to negative emotional health. Food addiction happens in two ways: those who overfeed on these comfort foods and then those who get their pleasure from not eating at all.

If you have read physical health journals and articles in relation to food, you likely encountered a the word "anorexic, : which refers to an eating disorder that makes people super conscious about their weight and what they eat. This is the very extreme end of what I am asking you to do today. And the reason I am really going in depth with this is because people have a tendency to replace one unhealthy habit with another unhealthy habit. So, if I say pay attention to what you eat, it is quite possible that to escape your emotional turmoil, you might fixate on the role that food plays in your mental well-being and possibly take things to the extreme.

To avoid that, I have decided to educate you on what could possibly go wrong if you find yourself taking things to the extreme. In cases involving anorexia, sufferers either sustain themselves with very little food in their bid to maintain their weight or they do what is generally referred to as a binge-purge where they consume a lot of food and then force themselves to immediately rid the food from their system by either sticking their hands down their throats to make them vomit or taking laxatives. This form of unhealthy food relationship also leads to health complications which can be fatal. Sufferers also get trapped in a cycle that is similar to the one we talked about earlier.

Now even if you do not belong to either group, it is important that you start giving more thought to the food you eat. Instead of just eating to survive, make it your mission to eat to thrive. Paying attention to what you eat requires you to be more conscious about what you eat and when you eat it. It also means eating the type of food that is best for you. For instance, if you have a medical condition like diabetes, there are certain foods that are simply off limits for you. In other words, what constitutes as healthy for some other person may not be right for you.

So, to kick start this process, go over your recent health records and if you don't have those, now would be a good time to talk to your health care provider. Know your current health status and discuss your options with your doctor. Don't make the mistake of jumping on the trendiest diet fad without proper consultations with your doctor. While your intentions may be good, the outcome could prove to have little benefit for your body. If you are given a clean bill of health, the best diet you can go on is a balanced diet.

A balanced diet ensures that you get the right amount of all the nutrients you need and you get those nutrients in the right daily proportions. If you are already on a restrictive diet like being a vegetarian, you will have to work hard at making sure that you make up for those aspects of your diet that are missing. Top up the protein that is missing in your diet. Red meat has its benefits, but it does not mean that if you are not eating red meat, you won't be able to enjoy those merits.

If you choose to go the diet route, like the Whole 30, which focuses on eliminating certain foods from your diet for a whole month and then reintroducing them later on, or maybe your nutritionist recommends the DASH [an acronym for dietary approaches to stop hypertension] diet, which is a salt-free diet, it is important your diet includes fruits and vegetables. They are vital for your physical and emotional well-being. Taking an active role in controlling what goes into your body can give you a good confidence boost. However, be cautious when setting the bar for your expectations for results. Don't expect to morph into the perfect body size after each meal or presume that your health status will dramatically change overnight.

The goal is not to transform your body; rather, the aim is to cultivate healthy eating habits that would serve you in the long term. However, this should not stop you from enjoying the benefits when they eventually come. Also, do not be afraid to stop a diet if you notice that the effect it has on you is affecting your health negatively. While some diets may boast of many great health benefits, it does not exactly guarantee that it is going to be the right fit for you. Be open to exploring diets, start with the ones recommended to you by your doctor or nutritionist. Chances are, you will find the best diet for you from their lists. Most importantly, have fun with your meals. Being on a diet is not necessarily boring.

DAY 12

Develop Your Own Mantra

If you are an avid follower of Hinduism or Buddhism, you are probably familiar with the word "mantra." Essentially, a mantra is comprised of words or sounds that repeated during meditation to help you focus. The long and protracted "ohm" sound is one of the most popular meditation mantras. They are a very important part of the meditation routine. However, for this task today, mantra takes on a different meaning, as I am not really talking about meditation. The mantra I am referring to has more to do with shaping your life and mindset in this phase. And today, you and I are going to work on allowing you to discover your power mantra.

When you start up a company, one of the things you need to work on is branding. This helps your customers identify you from the sea of choices available to them. A lot of the work that goes into the branding of a company is more focused on the aesthetic aspect. These companies strive to influence the market's opinion of them with the help of logos, brand colors as well as the fonts used in all of their marketing materials. However, the element that really defines how the company operates is tan organization's motto. In the same vein, the clothes you wear, the way you wear your hairstyle and all the physical stuff are just aspects of personal branding.

You can use your style to influence people's perception of you. But the thing that really defines how you interact with people, reacts to situations and generally carry yourself is strongly influenced by your personal beliefs. When we hear beliefs, we start thinking religion and culture. And to be honest, our religion and customs heavily influence our behaviors, but think about this for a second. If our beliefs were really rooted in our religion and culture, there is a very strong possibility that people who share the same customs would be more like replicas from a factory than the unique individuals that we are.

The differentiating factor for us is what we believe in personally. And even though you may not have given it a definition yet, the fact is you have a mantra. When you do not make the conscious effort to choose the mantra that defines you, life and everything else that happens to you will make that decision for you. And this is one of the reasons why many people are trapped in a destructive emotional cycle. There is a popular saying that if you don't stand for something, you will fall for everything. Today, you have to take the bold step of defining you. The mistakes you made in the past, the failures that you are living through in the present as well as your fears and concerns for the future are aspects of choices you make that have affected or will affect you. But they do not define you.

In the previous chapter, we talked about the "you are what you eat" phrase. Like aesthetics, this premise influences one aspect of you. Mantras are like your mental food. And because we know how strongly the mind influences our behavior, this makes a great case for choosing to define yourself. And now that we have established that, we have to go to the next step which is selecting the mantra.
Mantras in this context could be anything from a favorite celebrity quote to something culled from your favorite ancient Greek philosopher. Whatever you choose, do not fall for that socially trendy type of quote just because you feel people would think it is cool. Like with everything that has to do with your emotional wellbeing, the final decision is up to you. From the moment you were born, there are several voices competing for a space in your head. These voices are telling you how to do things, how to live your life and basically how to exist.

Now is your opportunity to create and horn in on your own voice. Let this voice take root deep within you and drown out every other belief system or voices that have held you down. The mantra should resonate with your innermost thoughts and desires. That is how you can tell that you are on the right track. It does not have to be "deep". But it should be something that every time you hear the words or speak the words, it changes your countenance for the better. Something as simple as "you are powerful" may be all you need to put your confidence together.

You can also have a mantra for different situations. Like if you are going to be making a presentation at work or maybe you have to speak in front of a crowd, you could choose a mantra that gives you the courage to step up and own the stage you are given. For times when you are experiencing some emotional lows which are very common if you are combating any of the negative emotions we talked about in the beginning, you can find mantras that will empower you to keep the darkness at bay.

When you find the right mantra, the next thing you might be thinking is how often you would need to say those words for them to have any effect. The only correct answer to that question is "as often as you need it." An old friend of mine used to reiterate, "motivation is like a bath: you need it every time you get dirty". And I agree with him 100%. Your mantra is not going to be a one-time-fix-it type of word that you just say, snap your fingers and everything falls into place. I wish there was a word or phrase like that but until that word has been discovered or invented, you are going to have to do your own behavioral conditioning every time you think you need it.

Say the words with conviction. Repeat them in sequence if you have to, but ensure that you are rooted in these words every day. As you evolve, you may have to take on new mantras. But you should always have that mantra that defines you no matter what. Find those words, speak those words, own those words and become those words. It would take a while for you to get there, but for today, let us settle for activating the inner victor within you with your own words!

Day 13

Practice Relaxed Breathing

Breathing is one of those reflexive activities that we take for granted every day. When a healthy baby is born, his or her first instinctive reaction is to fill up their lungs with air by simply inhaling and the same breath that they exhale, they release their first cry. Breathing is one of aspect that characterizes our nature, but we never truly realize the importance of this until a time comes when our breathing is compromised. Now don't panic because I know that the opening of this introduction sounds like a prelude to a doomsday warning. On the contrary, what I am trying to say is that there is more to breathing than merely inhaling oxygen and expelling carbon dioxide.

Earlier on we talked about the benefits of meditation and how we can use this to influence our emotional health positively and one of the things that people use to channel their focus during meditation is their breathing. This here is taking things to the next level. While the concept of relaxed breathing may sound like one of those new age mumbo jumbos, the truth is this is something that has been around for a while now. The use of relaxed breathing in modern medicine dates back to the 70s. However, my research reveals that this has been in existence for much longer.

Before you write off relaxed breathing as a wonky hack, here are some of the wonderful benefits of relaxed breathing:

1. It helps you to de-stress by filling your body up with oxygen and then getting your heart rate back to normal when your anxiety levels are sky high.
2. It plays a role in detoxifying your body by using those deep breaths to make your organs and systems more efficient at ridding the body of toxins.
3. On those days when your energy levels drop low on the scale, you can use relaxed breathing to give yourself an energy boost.
4. You can give your heart a good workout when you do those deep breathing exercises.
5. You can regulate your weight and burn fat with deep relaxed breathing.

With the kind of benefits, you would wonder why people aren't talking about this as much as they should. Chances are, they have been talking about this. You just haven't been paying any attention. Since our focus is on getting you to change your habits to improve your emotional well-being, we are going to capitalize on the emotional benefits of relaxed breathing.

Stress is one of life's experiences that we cannot escape. The source of stress for everyone is different as is our tolerance level for stress.

However, when stress is triggered in our bodies, our biological and emotional reactions are similar. The physical reaction to stress can range from headaches to a drastic drop in sex drive. Emotionally, you could experience anxiety and anger outbursts. Some people become withdrawn when they are under stress and this can lead to depression.

We can't stop stress. It comes with the territory of life. But, you can stop the adverse emotions that are usually a byproduct of stress in their tracks. The normal breathing for most adults is usually shallow breaths that do not go past their chests. Deep breathing goes all the way down to your abdomen. It does not have an aesthetically pleasing effect as it gives you a puffer fish appearance with the blown out tummy and all. But this is the only way you can get the most out of your breathing. When in a heightened emotional state due to stress, instead of reacting to those emotions, you can reduce them down to reasonable limits.

So, the next time you feel a rage bubble coming on and you want to let it out by lashing out at the nearest person or thing, take a deep gulp of air and then let it out slowly. Focus on your breathing when you do this. When we are upset, we take shorter breaths and this limits the diaphragm's range of motion causing a restriction of oxygenated air to the lower parts of the lungs. The physical manifestation of this is anxiety. Deep breathing helps you cultivate a healthy response to stress. One of the healthier responses to stress is called the "relaxation response."

According to the Harvard journal that was referenced for the research on this subject, relaxation response is a state of profound rest. Meditations, yoga as well as repetitive incantations or prayers have been known to induce this relaxation response. Another simple yet effective way to kick start this response is deep breathing. By focusing on your breath, you can guide yourself into extricating your emotions from your thoughts and entering into this state of profound rest.

Deep breathing sounds pretty straight-forward but there is more to it than just taking puffs of air. To get it right, what you first need to do is to take yourself immediately away from the source of the stress. Even if you are in a workplace, distance yourself from the stressful work or the stressful coworker. You may be tempted to react immediately but that is only going to worsen the situation. Instead, find a quiet and isolated space, just like you would if you were going to meditate. Get a good spot to either sit or lie down. Being on your back is preferable, but you can still get good results from a sitting position.

When you are in position, take a normal breath. Then, inhale slowly through your nose and let your chest as well as your lower belly rise as you do so. This fills up your lungs with air. Next, breathe out slowly through your mouth. Keep your focus on your breathing and repeat this until you start to feel the tension slowly slip out of your body. Once you have practiced and nailed this breathing technique, initiate it any time you feel stressed in any way. Getting yourself to calm down on the brink of a blowout is a habit that will pay off eventually in the long run.

While there are plenty of benefits to this, there is one downside. If you have a history of respiratory problems, you should talk to your doctor about this as this may cause complications in unsupervised situations.

Day 14

Gain Mastery Over Your Emotions

In the days leading up to your second week on this journey to reclaiming your life, I am very certain that you have been equipped with knowledge that ensures you can now accurately distinguish your emotions. And if you have religiously followed the daily steps that have been listed out so far, you have a fair handle on your emotions. The exercise you did yesterday is about learning to get your emotions under control. Today, I would like to push you to take things further. Instead of just putting a lid on your emotions, you can master them.

The emotions that we talked about in the beginning, the anger, the depression, fear and anxiety…these are intense emotions that can threaten to overpower you when they are being experienced at their peak. What you have been practicing so far acts as a barrier reef that stops the wave of emotions from crashing over and completely destroying you. Another thing we addressed with these emotions is that they have a positive side to them. Anger serves to embolden you to stand up for your right and what you believe. Anxiety and fear are your instinctive defensive mechanisms to protect you when you are threatened while depression and sadness help you cope with loss.

Shutting these emotions out would compromise your total wellbeing because without them, you make yourself extremely vulnerable. Conflicts, crisis, calamities and chaos are things that we will all experience more than once in our lives. These emotions are all part of living. And these negative emotions are there to help you navigate through those kinds of situations. Therefore, pushing back those emotions only serves you temporarily. In the early stages of this journey, it was more important to build your mental and emotional foundations before letting the dark emotions in. Now, you are ready to confront your demon so to speak.

In this chapter, we will address each emotion discussed in the first 5 chapters of this book and then look at how you can channel your reaction to them to serve you better. Unlike the green Hulk from the famous Marvel comics, we are not trying to lock the "monster" away. Oh no. we want the monster to step into your world. Only, you will be the one at the driver's seat. Don't fret and worry about losing control. This is something that may start off a little difficult for you, but with practice and consistency, it is certainly something that you can do.

Anger
Anyone who has ever reacted to their anger in a fit of rage will know that anger can be quite

venomous. Its effect on both the person who is angry as well as the person who is on the receiving end of that anger can be likened to that of a hurricane. It has been known to sever relationships, tear down empires, and lead to wars between nations. But, did you also know that it can inspire creativity? Some of the greatest movements that altered the course of humanity were inspired by anger.

In other words, anger can be used to your advantage. Next time when you feel a rage ensuing, use the techniques you have learnt so far bring the violent bubbles down to a gentle simmer and then do the following;

1. Get to the root of the anger. Don't react to the sting. React to the cause of the sting instead. You are bound to get more positive results this way.

2. Pick your battles carefully. When you are angry, something you value has been violated. Often times, those things are minor and not worth the hassle over. So, just breathe and ignore. In turn, you conserve energy for the things that matter.

3. Own your feelings. Sweeping things under the rug to present a façade of calmness can lead to a rage eruption of volcanic proportions somewhere down the road. In the very least, admit to yourself that you are angry and look for

constructive ways to express your feelings.

Anxiety

Fear activates your survival instincts. It is your body's way of telling you that it wants to live. Experts tell us that without the right amount of anxiety, there is a strong possibility that we will be complacent in how we live our lives. A complete lack of it would cause us to become reckless in our dealings. The instinct to look before we leap would be absent and so we would constantly find ourselves in situations that compromise our emotional and physical wellbeing.

Too much of it on the other hand can paralyze us completely. We would become paranoid about everything and become incapable of enjoying the simplest joys in life. To gain mastery over anxiety, you must first embrace the positives that it brings to you. Now whether your fears are real or imagined, you should never let them shut you down. Instead of reacting to your fear, act on it. Make a conscious decision to do something.

Depression

This emotion forces you to reflect on your pain. There is a general opinion that nothing positive can come from your reflections when you are depressed. In contrast, there are psychologists who believe that this might actually be good for you. This is because in sadness, you are in a better position to analyze what is really important to you than you would in a happier frame of mind.

Bearing this in mind, you can use your sadness to horn in the important things in your life by asking the right questions. The usual self-pity party question of "why me?" does not count. Using questions involving "what" and "how" can help you determine the problem as well as develop solutions to them.

Negative thoughts
This applies to everything on each of these three emotions. The upside to negative thoughts is that it brings your imperfections to the forefront. We may like to think of ourselves as perfect but alas, we are human. Dwelling on those negative thoughts is where the harm comes in from. Instead, embrace those things that you don't like about yourself. Improve on them if you can. But do not let that be the focus of your thoughts. Change your perspective about these emotions that haunt you and then you will be able to rewrite the narrative. This is how you gain mastery over your emotions today.

Day 15

Step Things Up with New Relaxation Techniques

So far, you have practiced meditation to clear your mind, deep breathing to induce relaxation response, and taken on a new outlook on those emotions that were once hanging over you like dark clouds. Accordingly, these techniques have given you a new lease on life, but the journey is far from over. While what you are doing might offer some relief in the short term, you need what I call "booster shots" to get you through to the long term. Right up until this moment, we have been dealing with the things that colored your past and activated those emotions in the first place. Now, we need to start working on habits that will fortify you against what might happen in the future.

You may have an army of psychics that can predict the future for you but we do know that those predictions do not offer absolute certainty. They are all just possibilities, a series of might or might not happen events. The only certainty in life is change. Things are always changing. Circumstances will always evolve. Things may seem bad now, but it will get better and then somewhere down the future, it will get bad again. Of course, situations might never repeat themselves. But, you have to brace yourself because you will be presented with new challenges. The fairytales from our storybooks always end with stories of living happily ever after, yet real life has a different version.

The uncertainties about the future should not force you to live in fear of tomorrow. That kind of behavior is what got you into this mess in the first place. The right thing to do would be to equip yourself with knowledge and habits that will build you up emotionally so that when the time comes, you are better able to deal with the situations and not fall back into the destructive cycle we have already discussed. Unfortunately, there are no spells or potions that can quickly zap us into emotionally stable individuals. But that is all part of the fun. They say that it is not about the destination, it is about the journey. In this case, the process that gets you to becoming even more is vital!

There are many relaxation techniques that are practiced in different parts of the world. Some of them have been in existence for centuries and perhaps are only just being discovered because of the world gradually becoming a small place. What this tells us is that mankind has always been concerned about their emotional wellbeing. Their source of anxiety may have been different from the experiences that we have today, but the threat remains nonetheless. There was a time that the most efficient way to deal with emotional traumas might have involved pills and a trip to the electric chair.

Thankfully, those times have changed. Through cultural integration, we are now being gifted with knowledge of how we can manage our emotions and force ourselves to relax in a world that seems to run on constant frenzy.

There are several additional relaxation techniques out there, and I encourage you to take explore them. However, our focus for today's exercise is going to be yoga.

Yoga
Yoga is all about finding your balance and serenity. Through a series of breathing exercises and body movement, you can consciously cause your mind and body to rest. Beyond relaxing you, if you find yourself in an energy rut which typically happens at the end of a long hard day, yoga can relax your nerves and leave you feeling reinvigorated.

Yoga has different poses that offer specific benefits. And because our goal is to help our minds and body relax, we are going to be looking at 5 poses that serve this purpose.

1. The Child Pose also known as Balasana
In this pose, you rest your chest and abdomen on your knees/ thighs with your feet stretched out behind you and your hands in front of you. Let your forehead touch the mat. This pose strengthens your breathing and has a calming effect. Remember to do it on an empty stomach.

2. The Reclining Fish Pose also known as Supta Matsyendrasana

Here you lay on your back with arms stretched out on either side of you at shoulder height. With one leg stretched out in front of you, cross the other leg over the outstretched one moving only the hip and that leg. Turn your face in the opposite direction of the crossed leg and hold position for 30-60 seconds.

3. The Legs up the Wall Pose also known as Viparita Karani

Just as the name implies, this pose requires you to place both legs on the wall as you lie flat on the ground with your arms stretched out on either side at shoulder height. In addition to relaxing you, it functions as a very mild form of anti-depressant. It is usually best for mornings.

4. The Corpse Pose also known as Savasana

All morbid thoughts aside, lay flat on your back with arms and legs apart. Stay still and just focus on breathing. This pose is simple but very effective for inducing rest. It is great for post workout as it soothes sore muscles and helps stimulate blood circulation.

5. The Bound Angle Pose also known as Supta Baddha Konasana

On your back, raise your hands above your head. Let the back of your hands touch the floor and let your thumbs and forefingers connect. And then bend your legs until your feet are facing each other and touching. Hold this pose for 30-60seconds. This pose keeps headaches, panic attacks and muscle fatigue at bay. It is also useful for lowering your blood pressure.

These are all beginner poses and are pretty simple to do. As you grow, you can extend the time period and perhaps explore more advanced yoga poses that offer the same benefits to this. While you are in each pose, you can also do your deep breathing exercises to make the most of things. This would amplify the results that you get. Also bear in mind that this is not a one off thing. It is something that you should practice and get comfortable doing almost every day. While you are at it, you can also research other relaxation techniques like Taichi. Every information you acquire and practice can go on to building a stronger foundation for your emotional wellbeing.

Day 16

Reflect on the Experience

There is a general misconception about communication. We assume that the most difficult people to communicate with are others...as in the people in our lives. But in the true sense of things, communication with ourselves is what we find most difficult. This is because when it comes to ourselves, objectivity is usually missing. If someone other than ourselves were going through circumstances that are similar to our own and we are called to weigh in, we would probably be spot on with our emotional assessment of the situation and perhaps even offer actionable solutions. But when it comes to us, we either run around in circles or worse, crash into brick walls.

This is because we often lack the objectivity required to see things as they are because we are clouded by our own feelings and emotions. To be objective, you need to change your perspective and that can only happen with self-reflection. Now self-reflection is quite different from just simply sitting down at thinking of the situation. Brooding on a situation drags you deeper into the maze of your emotions. Self-reflection on the other hand purposefully analyzes and applies a practical solution. In other words, it is a form of self-assessment. This is a place where you get to be 100% honest with yourself.

In the past, you have needed to put the blame on others so that you could ensure the day. To move forward, that kind of thinking can no longer apply. Whether the blames assigned to the different people is justified or not, it is important that you acknowledge your role in the event. Mind you, this is not about assigning the blame to yourself either. That ship has sailed. This is reflecting on the process that brought you to this point, retracing your steps, reclaiming your power and redefining the impact this experience will have on you. We don't realize how powerful our mind is but all of that is about to change today.

When you are self-reflecting on an experience, you are not going back to the past as a victim or a victor. You are not trying to create and then sell a narrative that you feel will pacify your wounded emotions. You are revisiting this past as an observer and nothing more. Yes, you have lived with the pain and yes, you bear the scars but you are not bound to hold on to those. Revisit the moment or event where you think you lost everything, trace the steps that brought you to that event and then follow up on what happened after the event to where you are today. Again, try not to dwell on the "why" questions. It is harder to get the answers to those if other people are involved. However, if this event itself is something you can classify as self-inflicted, then you can most certainly try to analyze why you did it.

Now, bearing in mind that you cannot change what has happened, you would have to accept the situation for what it is before moving on the next set of questions which would center around how you could have done things differently. The purpose for this line of questioning to determine how you can avoid situations like that in the future. This would prevent you from repeating the same mistake. I have to emphasize here again that this is not the time to assert blames. Acknowledging your role in the event and then assigning blames are two different things. One paves the way for redemption, while the latter breeds guilt and self-destruction.

During this phase, assess your strengths and your weaknesses. This kind of knowledge empowers you to make the right and relevant changes that you need. With this newly acquired knowledge of yourself, if you are ever confronted with similar circumstances, there is a very high possibility that you will make better choices. And the beautiful thing about these choices that you will make subsequently is that they are not rooted in fear or any other negative emotions. But rather, they are being made objectively which would mean that the results would be beneficial for the long term. The lessons acquired will educate the steps that you would take in the future.

Now that you have done your self-assessment in relation to the experience, you can now reduce the impact that the experience would have over you. Let me use a practical example here. I know someone who had been in a relationship for almost 13 years. They met in their early college years and sustained that relationship until they entered the job market. I will call the lady "Laura" because she is the one I know. For Laura, this relationship was her first and only one at the time. And because they had been together for so long, she assumed that this union was going to her happily ever after. She built her hopes and dreams around this relationship only for her prince charming to end things abruptly in what would have been their 13th year together. You can imagine how devastated Laura was. For months, she suffered from depression and panic attacks.

I met Laura during this time, and we began working on turning things around. When we got to this point, Laura noted her fear of rocking the boat in a relationship and how it prevented her from asking the right questions that would have saved her time and heartache. Instead of jumping on the "all men are scum" wagon. Her self-assessment helped her open herself up to new relationship prospects and informed the choices that she made going forward. She took out a year to date herself and in the year following that, she got involved with a pretty decent bloke. Today, she is married and living out her new dreams. The moral lesson here is not that she found happiness. It was the deliberate choices that she was able to make thanks to her objective assessment of her experience. Today, pick up a pen and book and go down memory lane as well.

Day 17

Focus on the Good

Remember that gratitude list that you started some days back? Well, now we are about to step things up. I assume that it is safe to say that you may have heard or come across the "glass half full" expression. This is used to illustrate what a positive outlook and a negative outlook on life are like. They say that the optimistic person would always look at a glass that has liquid in it that is halfway to the top as half full while the pessimistic guy would look at the same glass as half empty. It all boils down to perspective. The perspective we have about life to a large extent would determine our experiences.

Contrary to what we think, our perspective of life is neither genetic nor hereditary. It is a choice that we make and one that we have to continuously make. Sometimes, life's experiences condition us to think and react in a certain way. If you have had a slew of negative experiences thrown at you, it is quite understandable if you begin to develop a fear that some kind of doom or tragedy is awaiting you at every corner. However, even in situations like these, you can make the choice to see things through a brighter lens. Becoming optimistic is the goal, but that is not something that is going to happen over the weekend. It starts with a small but very significant step...seeing the good in everything!

Realists may struggle with this more than pessimists because realists tend to focus on grander things. A realist is not so impressed by the penny that they find on the ground because they think that it might feed their fear of deluding themselves. The sun peeking from beneath dark angry looking clouds is not enough to give them hope about the rains being averted. Those dark clouds would have to go before they would entertain any thought of hope. Whether you are a pessimist, a realist, or an optimist, you have to start training yourself to see the good, no matter how small.

Just to clarify things, this is not to say that you should ignore the bad things or be dismissive of them. It is about getting a balanced perspective. In every situation, there is always a silver lining. Sometimes it is harder to find that rainbow in the midst of your storm but if you keep at it, I guarantee that you will find it. When I was taking this journey during a very painful period in my life, I used to feed my "good sight" with common internet clichés. Initially, they sounded really terrible and unhelpful but as I repeated them, I began to notice positive changes in how I viewed this. I bring this experience up because seeing the good things isn't always about sight. It was in how I reacted to things as well as how I perceived situations.

Focusing on the good things in your life is a deliberate attempt to reclaim hope in a situation that brings you despair and there are very few things that are as powerful as that. Another effective way to focus on the good is to redefine the negative. For instance, if anger is a problem that you are struggling with, instead of hanging on to the negative label that characterizes such behaviors, give yourself a positive spin on things. Choose instead to see yourself as a person who is intensely passionate about things that matter to you and right now, you are trying to figure out how to constructively express your passion in a way that everyone around you can benefit from it. This is not self-denial. But rather, it is a more productive way to help you reclaim your hope and motivate yourself to make the relevant changes.

A study was conducted on the subject of silver lining and it was discovered that 90% of people who were able to convince themselves that their negative traits were strengths were more motivated to work harder to attain the positive attributes of those strengths. This right here is science. Like I said earlier, it is amazing what you are able to achieve when you set your mind to it.

One theme I have repeated throughout this book is the fact that you have to accept the situation for what it is. You cannot go back in time to change what has happened but you can reach into the future to change how it will affect you now. To do this, you need to make some projections. What would you like to see happen? What are the things about your situation that if they changed would make you happier and feel more grateful for life? Now picture yourself in the future with those things and the outcome you have projected. With this in mind, come back to the present. Now, ask yourself, what are the things you think you can do now that would give you the outcome that you desire? Create a plan that would lead you to that point, write it down in clear and concise words and then run with it. This is another way to focus on the good.

These little thoughts of good help you redirect your focus and give you something to look forward to. When we feel like we have nothing to live for, the darkness and the negativity would take over and bring us to the pit. This does not have to be your story. Whether you are redefining yourself, reaching to the future or just feeding your 'good sight," you have to actively make the decision to stay in the light every day. The future is uncertain, but when you envelope yourself in positivity, there is almost no mountain that you cannot climb to get to your destination. It is time to stop letting things happen to you. Get up and start happening to the things around you. It is easy to shrug your shoulders and say life happened but don't. Look into the mirror, shrug your shoulders and say "you happened" instead.

Day 18

Uproot the Negative Sources

There is a Christian parable about a farmer sowing his seeds. Some of these seeds fell on hard soil, so they were scorched by the sun and unable to grow. Some fell on fertile soil and of course they grew, bloomed and bore fruits. And then you have the seeds that fell among thorny bushes. The farmer tried to grow, but the bushes and thorns choked the life out of them and so they withered and died away. Trying to be optimistic when you are surrounded by negativity is akin to planting seeds among thorns and bushes. The negativity would choke the life from the little light and hope you have tried to carve out for yourself leaving you with the darkness.

But like everything else, this too is a choice. You have taken the bold step to redefine yourself and your purpose in life. Now you will have to take an even bolder step to get rid of anything that brings negativity into your life and sometimes that includes people. It is funny how some of these types of negative people in our lives convince themselves that they are only speaking the truth. They use clichés like "the truth hurts" or "the truth is always bitter" to justify the mean things that they say to you. Some people don't even come outright with the mean words. They use snarky comments and backhanded statements to throw you off your game. Today, all of that ends.

It is not your job to try to figure out where their bitterness is coming from (you better believe that they have a source), but you owe it to yourself to look out for yourself first. So, if you have toxic personalities in your life, you are going to have to eliminate them or at the very least tune out their voices. It is very important that you take a very vicious approach to cutting negative people out of your life because the amount of energy required to dismantle the negative impact of toxic words is more than three times the energy required for you to develop a new positive habit. If you choose to tolerate those type of people in the name of maintaining friendships, you would find yourself expending energy in undoing the damage that they do daily instead of living your life. And on top of everything, they are not the only negative voices you are going to have to silence.

The second negative source in our lives is usually found within you. When you have battled with situations that compromised your confidence and left you emotionally battered, it awakens a voice within. The voice of self-doubt. Even when you make giant strides in achieving your goals, you would still hear this voice screaming out from the recesses of your mind telling you that you cannot do it. Sometimes, the piercing screams of our self-doubt can have a paralytic effect on us. This would leave you stuck in murky waters which would then distract you from the other amazing things you could and should be doing. To drown out the voices of self-doubt, you would have to activate another voice. Remember those mantras you have been practicing, you would have to kick things up a notch. Listen to the words that the voice of self-doubt is saying and look for mantras that counter those words positively. The more empowered they make you feel, the better for you.

Outside the voices of self-doubt, you are going to have to banish other negative thoughts that may have been programmed by your beliefs, culture and so on. What you believe in has a very strong hold over you. I have heard the phrase, "a man of conviction is a dangerous man." In other words, because someone like that is firmly rooted in what he or she believes, so shaking this person is going to be as effective as using a regular razor blade to cut through solid steel. Your belief forms a solid wall that is much akin to the steel I used in the illustration. To cut through it, you would need more positive affirmations as well as the redefinition of certain opinions you have held about some things.

You would also need a ton of sheer will power to push through. Today, you will be exerting a lot of mental effort as you attempt to put your life in order. Think of it as preparing your soil for the planting season ahead. If there are habits, materials or images that feed the negativity that surrounds you, it is imperative that you are brutal in eliminating them. Don't let sentiments stand in the way. Somethings or people may be easily let go of perhaps due to familial relationships or some kind of obligation. Perhaps, the source of the toxicity in your life is your workplace but due to financial considerations, you are not in a position to sever ties immediately. In situations like this scenario, you can devise with an action plan to exit at a later time. So, even if you cannot extricate yourself right away, you have something to look forward to in the coming days.

I know I make it sound easier than it actually is but this would make a huge difference in everything. When you let go of anything that might compromise your peace of mind, you are contributing to the creation of an emotionally stable environment that nurtures this new person that you are trying to become. Even more than that, it helps you thrive. As you uproot the negative elements in your life, ensure that you replace them with more positives. Stock up on books that feed you emotionally. Write little positive phrases and quotes and strategically place them around your home and person. Stumbling on them at random moments can inject a much-needed confidence boost.

As you let go of negative friends, connect with people who inspire and motivate you. In this era of social media, you can opt to ensure that your timeline is filled with positive messages by following people who exude the type of content that resonates with you. Constantly remind yourself that you are in charge and you may not control what happens. However, you can control how you react to it and how much it affects you.

Day 19
Bring Positivity to Others

When you have been the recipient of something good, the next best thing is to pay it forward. In the last few days, you have benefited from the wisdom of others and I am not referring to the words in this book. I am talking about the mantras and the positive phrases that you have researched and adopted as your own are gifts from others who came before you. Today, you are going to try and sow back positive seeds into the world that has blessed you. Now this does not mean that you have to start sprouting words of wisdom for others to discern. However, there are things that you can do to get the ball rolling in that direction but first let us find out what this does for you.

If you have never done something selflessly for someone, I suggest you drop this book right now and try it. Beyond seeing the smile on the face of the person whom you are doing the good for, there is just a warm feeling that fills you up. Studies have shown that personal acts of kindness activate a part of your brain that decreases the effects of anxiety. Of course the results are not conclusive, but it is a very promising subject. Still, we are not going to wait until the results from that study are concluded before we act on it. Meeting the need of another human being is a fundamental aspect of human nature and this should be encouraged.

Secondly, doing acts of good draws you out of your own head. It doesn't take much to find yourself preoccupied with the problems that you face. We get so caught up in our own world so much that we forget that there is an entire universe filled with other human beings who are equally facing their own set of problems and even though they are not your responsibility, it helps to show a little empathy. Spending even just 5 minutes as a helpful listening ear might reveal how trivial your problem is in comparison. Don't feel the need to hog the spotlight when it comes to who life has been most unfair to. You may feel like you are the only one in the world, but all you have to do is reach out and you will be amazed to discover that there are so many people willing to fill up your life with love.

As a child, my grandfather gave me an illustration of generosity that stuck with me all of my life. We had gone on a fishing trip and then he asked me to reach into the basket and give him some bait. Just as I handed him the bait, my grandfather held my hand over his and said to me, "givers will always be on top." This image has always played in my mind all these years. When we think of giving, our worry is usually what we have to lose. That favorite sweater, that extra cash or even our time...we tend to think of it as a loss. But in reality, we are gaining so much more. And the more we give, the more we gain.

Giving back to the world is not as complicated as it sounds. And you don't need to go on a venture halfway across the world to be able to give. Charity, they say, begins at home. You can start in your home and then take things to your community. There are lots of ideas for giving and not all gifts have to involve you parting ways with cash. If you are short on inspiration, let my list give you a hint.

1. Volunteer your services:

Look for a cause that you are passionate about and then find an organization that supports that cause in your neighborhood. Most NGO are usually overwhelmed by the demand for the services that they offer so an extra set of helping hands are always welcomed. Offer to serve the organization in any capacity that you can. It does not have to be a long-term thing, so don't worry about making a commitment that you are not ready to accept.

The service you offer could be dependent on the type of organization you volunteered for. Medical NGOs would require medical personnel or at least someone with some medical background and educational organizations would require teachers. So, have this in mind when you make your application.

2. Volunteer your time:

Not all of us are keen on working with other people and if the idea of applying to an NGO puts you off, you can still do your bit for your community by donating minutes and hours of your time for community service. Perhaps the recreational park close to you is being invaded by trash. Get your gear, walk around the park and pick up the trash. You can choose to do this at your own convenience as well.

When volunteering your time, simply look out for opportunities that will show you how best you can use your time to help your community. Even taking the extra time to properly sort your trash at home can be of great benefit to yourself, the community, and the environment.

3. Random acts of kindness
If you are not going to be able to volunteer your time and/or your service, you need to jump on this wagon that lets you just pick sporadic moments to acts of kindness to anyone, despite if it's a known face or a complete stranger.

Giving up your seat for an elderly person on the bus or train, giving a warm and welcoming smile to your new co-worker or giving someone a genuine compliment...these are all acts of kindness.

Today, your task is to perform at least one good deed for someone other than family. Be creative in carrying out your task. Subsequently, make this a daily habit. Put out positive vibes to the universe and watch the universe respond in kindness.

Day 20

Live in the Moment

The present circumstances in your life may not be ideal and living through it might be a painful daily experience for you. But getting yourself stuck in a once glorious past or keeping your head in the clouds of a future that is not certain is not going to make things any better. When people give the advice to "live in the moment," we picture a life that has many good things going on for that person who just seems to be negligent of the "gifts" they possess. But for people who are living through one of the darkest times in their lives, that statement is a heavy burden to bear. It almost seems impossible to do. This is why a lot of people try to escape their lives through drugs, alcohol, and other harmful addictions.

Making the choice to live in the moment despite the tough circumstance surrounding you is a brave and courageous decision that I applaud. It would require more exercise of your will power to stay on track with this decision as there are so many distractions that can offer an escape. And even when you are able to stay away from the distractions, every now and then, you will encounter events that will cause you to become anxious and lead you to worry about the future. These concerns again take you away from the present and all of this can contribute to creating an atmosphere of despair. If you are not vigilant, you could become overwhelmed by it all and lose sight of what is important. Because, no matter how dark things get right now, your bright future is rooted in your ability to cease a moment in your present. And you can only recognize that moment if you are living in it. This is the paradox of life.

The first step to living in the present is to slow down your pace. Today's life is lived on the fast lane. We are always in a hurry to get to our destination. We look for short cuts to getting the job done. We want things to happen at the speed of light. The technology that is being created for this age is designed to meet our need for faster service. The irony is that in our hassle to get to where we are going to in the shortest time possible, we end up running around in circles. We become like those cute little hamsters on wheels. They just pedal and pedal but end up not really going anywhere. This is why they say, "It is not about the destination, it is the journey that counts". Don't be so focused on getting to your office on time that you ignore the important people and experiences on your way there. Hug your partner a little tighter before you head out the door. Give a hearty high five to the kids. Smile and wave at the neighbor as you head to your car. Take in the sights and sounds of the city as you navigate your way through traffic. Your job will still be waiting for you, but this moment slips away forever. Stop and smell the roses, literally and figuratively.

The next step is to be more mindful. What this means essentially is that you have to consciously pay more attention to what is happening around you right now. Life does not happen in reverse neither does it have a fast-forward button. It progresses with each waking moment. Your fears about the future should not disrupt your actions in the now. I am not implying that your concerns are not founded and that you should not plan for tomorrow. But don't get so caught up in those plans that you neglect what is going on right now. Make a deliberate effort to pay attention to the things you are doing now. Even if they are simple mundane activities that you do every day, focus your mind to stay on the task. For instance, when you sit down to have a meal, don't just go through the motions of putting the food in your mouth, chewing and then swallowing. Savor the taste and texture of the food. Celebrate the burst of flavors in your mouth and this may sound like you being extra but it really is just taking advantage of the moments in your life.

Finally, to truly live in the moment, you have to realign your priorities with your present realities. In every stage in our life, our priorities change but not many of us recognize this. What was important for you in your 20s may not hold the same value when you get to your 30s, but we hold on to this anyway. A typical example would be the value we place on our careers when we are single and then still choosing career over the other valuable things in our lives when we get married. This is not suggesting that your career has to be over when you get married and start a family of your own. But it is an undeniable fact that a shift in priority happens. Your family becomes your priority. Failure to do this would result in unnecessary conflicts that take away from the joy of living in the moment. This applies to every aspect of your life. You should give priority to what you place value on if you want to maximize the benefits of living in the present.

Another important factor that can ruin your ability to enjoy the present is keeping a judgmental attitude towards life. We reside in an era where everyone has an opinion about everything, and we all think we are right. To add fuel to an already burning flame, there are several social platforms that amplifies your opinions, so we are always eager to express our displeasure at every turn. The downside to this (among a million on my list) is that we become narrow-minded and intolerant when our myopic beliefs are echoed by strangers around the world. So, instead of approaching a moment with an open mind and open hands, we take on a critical stand thus missing out on the pleasures out there. It is vital to be rooted in our beliefs, to have a voice that represents our values, but it is even more important to live our lives with an open mind. Being open minded is what creates the opportunity for you to enjoy the surprises contained in these little moments that comprise our life's experiences.

Day 21
Letting it all go

To conclude what I know to have been an emotionally trying 3 weeks for you, I am proud that you are now "letting it all go." Not too long ago, you spent the day getting rid of any negative elements in your life, so it does beg the question of "what exactly are you letting go today?" The answer is quite simple. Today is the day that you let go of the pain. Now, this realization offers some good news, right? I mean, no one wants to carry his or her pain around 24/7. If there is a chance to physically exorcise yourself of the emotional pain we feel, a lot of us would sign up for it in a heartbeat. But if we are given the chance to let go of the pain freely, many of us would hesitate. This hesitation is not because we enjoy the pain. It is because on a subconscious level, we have bonded with our pain and this has become our identity. Letting go is one of the hardest things to do, which is why I reserved it for the last tip. But it is also the most significant step to take in getting you to move on with your life mindfully and healthily.

Holding on to the pain from the past and trying to tap into the future is like making omelet with rotten eggs. You have all the ingredients needed for an omelet but putting something that is already contaminated ruins all the taste and flavors that the other ingredients give even though they are in good condition. The only thing you should hold onto from your past is the lessons you've acquired. The pain taught you the lessons, but it is not the pain that will transform your life. It is the lessons. Clutching the pain will just ruin any wonderful experiences you may have going forward. The exercises you have been doing in the last few weeks have been preparing you for this moment. It is scary for sure, but it is also one of the bravest things you can do today.

To help with the scary part, instead of idealizing the pain, how about you put the power of your mind to work by redefining this moment. If letting go sounds a little too hard for you, let us call it the moment that you break up with pain. That sounds a lot better and puts a more positive spin on things. Now, let us get right into the business of it. Pain is not like a tangible thing that you can scoop up with a dustpan and then empty into the trash can. But, there are ways you can still achieve that same effect as you put things behind you with this step by step process.

Step 1: Stop petting the pain
Humans keep pets for various reasons but the most common reason is for companionship. When we feel sad and lonely, we reach out to our furry friends and pet them to make ourselves feel better. We let our pets absorb the feelings and draw on the unconditional love

they give us to improve our moods. Many of us treat our pain like pets. Every time something negative happens, we reach for that pain and use it to comfort ourselves. It is not a conscious thing that we do, but if you really want to move on, you are really going to have to stop pampering your pain.

Step 2: Stop making excuses

We know that this pain and bitterness we carry inside cannot bring anything good but every time it comes down to letting go, we start making excuses like "the pain is a reminder of what I have been through." Clichés like that sound like they are deep but in reality, they are just another excuse to retain your baggage. There are other great ways to remind yourself of this experience. Some people get tattoos, some people opt for engraved jewelry, and my favorite is the one where they choose a day in the year to commemorate the battle they fought and the well-earned victory that crowned their bravery. Whatever you choose to do, strive to ensure that you are embracing the right things for the right reasons.

Step 3: Stop playing the victim

We know that this tragic and terrible thing happened to you and that you don't deserve it, but wearing the victim badge just to garner sympathy from everyone is not going to help you move on in any way. For starters, the victim badge cancels out any scenario where you come out as the winner. The only thing it gets you is sympathy and even then, there is an expiry date for the sympathy you are getting now. This fleeting "reward" is not a good reason to cling on to an illusion where pain gets you what you want. This kind of thinking would work against all your effort to move forward. In relationships, you might become mistrustful and manipulative. People may stay with you based on sympathy, but you can only manipulate them for so long.

Step 4: Stop making comparisons

Putting your pain on a pedestal and then using that as a yardstick to define the events that happen to you going forward can make things get ugly really quick. No matter how beautiful you try to make that pedestal seem, it just won't work as long as you have that pain sitting up there. Think of the rotten egg in omelet analogy I used earlier. It doesn't matter if you put the fanciest ingredients in it. Sea salt, Moroccan spices or even the purest form of virgin olive oil cannot change the nasty flavor or smell that the rotten egg would bring to the meal. The same goes for letting pain define your future.

Today, make a conscious effort to let go of the pain. And as you do so, make it a point to forgive all the parties involved. And most prominently, forgive yourself. If you are harboring feelings of revenge, you need to let it go. Letting go does not mean that you are letting the other person off the hook. In fact, it is not really about them anymore. Letting go is about you and your emotional wellbeing. When you cling to a grudge or pain, you give that person or thing power over you. This journey is about reclaiming your power and rising above your emotional battles. No one and nothing should have that much power over you. Let it all go and watch yourself grow.

Embracing the Brand New You

Congratulations! You have made it thus far. I am really excited about the next phase of this journey that you are about to take. If you fell along the way, that is okay. We are not defined by our failures but by our ability to get back up every time we fall. In the last three weeks, you have really put yourself out there. You rode the storm, faced your fears and rewrote your story. You have awakened yourself to your true nature and you have gained knowledge that will continue to serve you for a very long time to come. I am also certain that you have managed to surprise yourself in this period. The revelations about yourself and your experiences in life have opened the door that has led to a more intimate relationship with yourself.

The unveiling of this new dimension to you is a remarkable experience. However, you are not done with this journey just yet. This is literally just the tip of the iceberg. The part of you that has just come up to surface extends deep beneath. As long as life keeps happening, you will need to keep at it. Everything you have learnt and practiced here needs to be repeated on a daily basis until it becomes a part of you. Get yourself to a point where you no longer need to do lists and phone reminders to tell you what to do and when to do it. It should become like breathing. You don't have to psyche yourself or remind yourself to take the next breath, you just do. Don't wait until there is a crisis to start another 3-week routine. Prepare yourself for those moments now so that when (those moments will always come) they arrive, you are in the best shape to take things on and get through it. Situations that would have previously seen you falling apart will now empower you to become even stronger.

As much as you would love this new you and cannot imagine being anyone else (except maybe Bill Gates or Beyoncé), it is essential that you keep an open mind because you will change. Some of those changes are inevitable and it is natural to resist it. But don't fight it for too long. Embrace those changes just as you have taken to this new you. Now while you are high fiving yourself on these milestones you are making, have a care for the people in your life. If the new you manifest this change physically as well as emotionally, it may reflect in your dress sense among other things. Perhaps you were the conservative type who wore muted colors and stayed away from bold graphical prints, you might find yourself being drawn to bright colors and bolder prints. This might be a bit of a shocker to people who know you, especially especially for those who share similar style sense with your previous style preferences. You need to give them some time to adjust to the new you.

Maybe you were the loud and boisterous type who lived an extroverted lifestyle but as you have gotten in touch with your true self, you realize that this is not you anymore. So, you become more introverted. Friends and family who have seen you in your finest extroverted hour would have a hard time reconciling that person they knew with this new person that you have become. You may have to be open to the possibility that they may not be entirely psyched about this new you right away. Don't try to change yourself just so that they can become comfortable with your transformation but don't force this new you down their throats either. Be patient with them and trust that they will come around eventually. As you continue to discover more layers to yourself, you should also do your best to balance the relationships in your life throughout the process. If balancing your relationships appear to be interfering with what you are trying to achieve, perhaps you should have a quick chat with them explaining what you are doing and why you may not be as accessible as you normally would. This quick chat will let them know that you trying to improve yourself and those who really love you can better support your efforts and encourage you to keep at it.

This is a period where you are permitted to be a little selfish. Your mental and emotional health is important. So even after you complete this three-week exercise, make it a point of duty to find time every day for yourself. You are in a better position to love and give positivity if you are able to stock up on self-love and positive energy. It is impossible to give what you don't have. Don't get sidetracked by "distractions." The Internet is a great resource for information, but if you don't make conscious decisions, you could end up being sucked into its endless maze of irrelevant and mindless data.

Teach yourself to practice joy every day. They say that happiness is a choice and given your newfound power in the choices you make, diligently seek out joy in everything that you do. You can do this by starting off each day with the mentality that every day that you wake up to is presenting you with a clean slate. Life will scribble a few things on that slate but the main author is you. And if it turns out that you don't like the narrative that life is giving, grab the pen and rewrite that chapter.

All of these things you are doing is to honor this new person that you have become. Love this amazing person that you are now. Don't settle for anything less than you deserve. Don't let this be a phase in your life. It should be a continuous process. Seek out new adventures, confront old fears…stay evolving. There is so much you have to live for and if you ever get stuck in a similar kind of emotional jam that drove you to this book in the first place, remind yourself of this. You have come a very long way, and there is a long road ahead. But if you can make it this far, you can go even farther.

I am confident in you and in all your efforts to making this transformation, so much so that I urge you to share your personal experience with others. Your story might uplift them and inspire them to claim their own power. Remember, it is in lifting other people that we lift our communities. Just like the many people who have inspired you to be better, you can be the inspirations for others.

On a final note, you do not have to wait until the start of the New Year to implement the changes that you want to see in your life. Every day is a good day and this is enough reason to get out of bed and march your way into your best life. New Year's resolutions are great and all, but new day resolutions are absolutely the hottest self-care trends to try at the moment.

Closing

I want to thank you so much for giving me the honor of including me on your journey. Thank you for letting me be one of the voices in your head that encourages you to be better. Being allowed into your space makes me feel truly blessed and humbled. I am usually eloquent with my words, but in moments like these, I lack the words that accurately encapsulates my thoughts and feelings. Suffice it to say, you inspire me!

It is my earnest desire to see that people are able to build relationships with themselves. There are too many broken people in the world: despite e the advent of the Internet and the wealth of information from technology, there is still not enough knowledge out there to help them heal from their wounds. Many of us have been rendered cripple emotionally and mentally by the tragedies that we have endured. We have gone from living to just surviving. We were made for more than that. I don't just want to live; instead, I want to thrive and I want these things for all of us!

Emotional healing starts from within and there is no surgery as of this moment that can fix that. However, in the face of this seemingly helpless situation, we have been given the power to turn things around for ourselves. The game changer in all of this is choice. What have you decided to do with your life today? Are you going to sit back and take everything that is being tossed your way? Or are you going to stand up and say "enough?" These are the choices that you are confronted with today, and your answer will determine the rest of your life.

I hope that you find the courage to choose life every day. No matter what the rest of the world has said about you, the simple truth is that you deserve better. And while you may have become isolated in your struggles, know that you are never alone. Millions of people around the world share stories that are similar to your life experiences. And many of them have done more than just survive those experiences. They have persevered on top. And the remarkable thing about their stories is that these victories they have didn't come by wealth or a change in their circumstances. It was as a result of a change in their attitude.

They recognized their power and they acted on it. The change did not happen overnight. And the change did not stop the moment they got their victory. It is a process that happens every day and they thrive in the fullness of it. The best part is that they do not have a monopoly on this. You can also rebuild from the loss you have experienced and restore relationships that have been damaged. Tragedy and trauma do not have to characterize your life. Choose instead to characterize those things that have gone wrong. You can transform your life in 21 days and there is no better time to begin this journey than now.

James W. Williams

For those who have started, I celebrate you in advance. Be consistent, be diligent, and most importantly, be deliberate!

Thank you

Before you go, I just wanted to say thank you for purchasing my book.

You could have picked from dozens of other books on the same topic, but you took a chance and chose this one.

So, a HUGE thanks to you for getting this book and for reading all the way to the end.

Now I wanted to ask you for a small favor. **Could you please consider posting a review on the platform? Reviews are one of the easiest ways to support the work of authors.**

This feedback will help me continue to write the type of books that will help you get the results you want. So if you enjoyed it, please let me know.

Lastly, don't forget to grab a copy of your Free Bonus book *"Bulletproof Confidence Checklist."* If you want to learn how to overcome shyness and social anxiety and become more confident, then this book is for you.

www.ingramcontent.com/pod-product-compliance
Lightning Source LLC
Chambersburg PA
CBHW071717020426
42333CB00017B/2298